WITH A CD OF PIANO ACCOMPANIMENTS

HIGH VOICE

WORSHIP SOLOS
FOR SINGERS

ISBN 978-1-4768-7729-7

Visit Hal Leonard Online at
www.halleonard.com

CONTENTS

PIANIST ON THE CD: HANK POWELL

Above All

Words and Music by PAUL BALOCHE
and LENNY LeBLANC

10
E♭
B♭/D
Cm7
You were here __ be - fore __ the world _ be - gan.

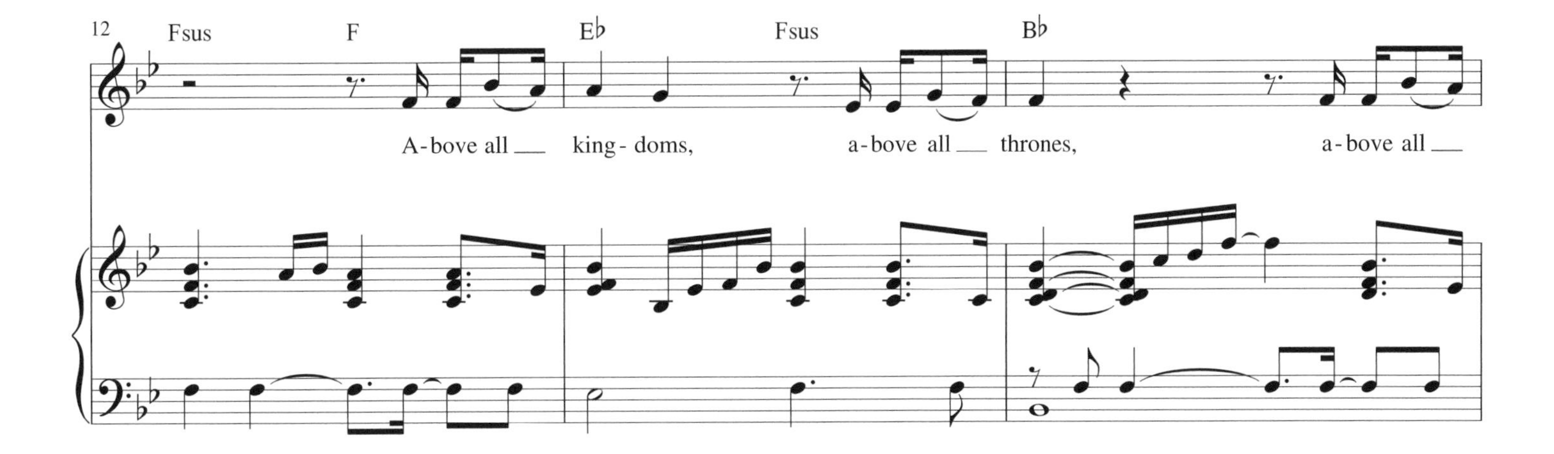
12
Fsus
F
E♭
Fsus
B♭
A-bove all __ king - doms, a-bove all __ thrones, a-bove all __

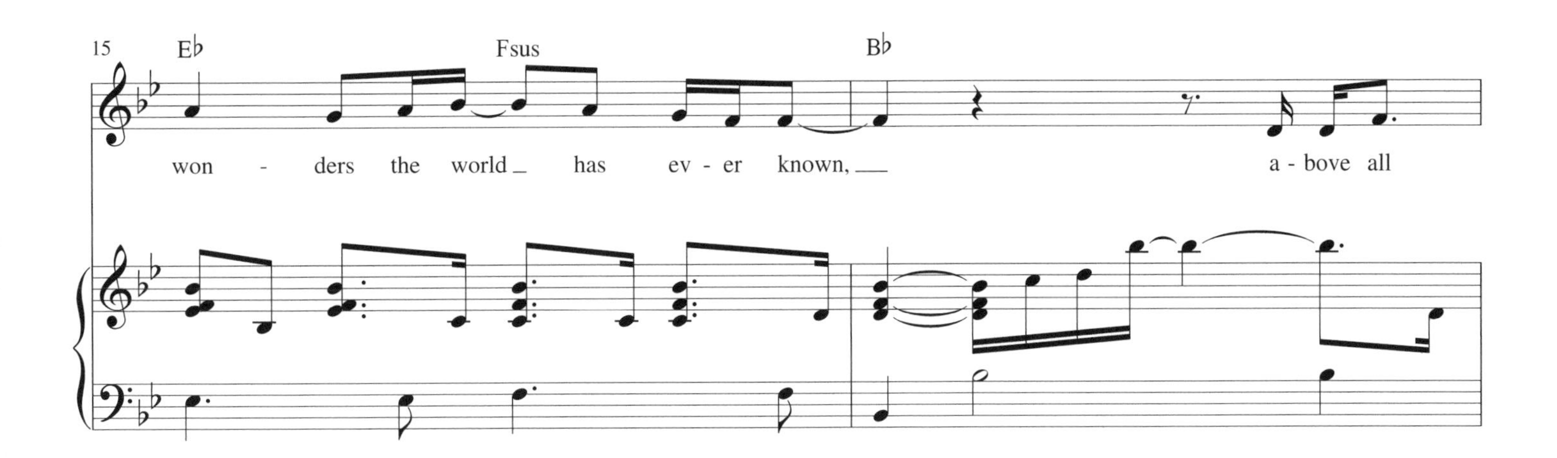
15
E♭
Fsus
B♭
won - ders the world _ has ev - er known, __ a - bove all

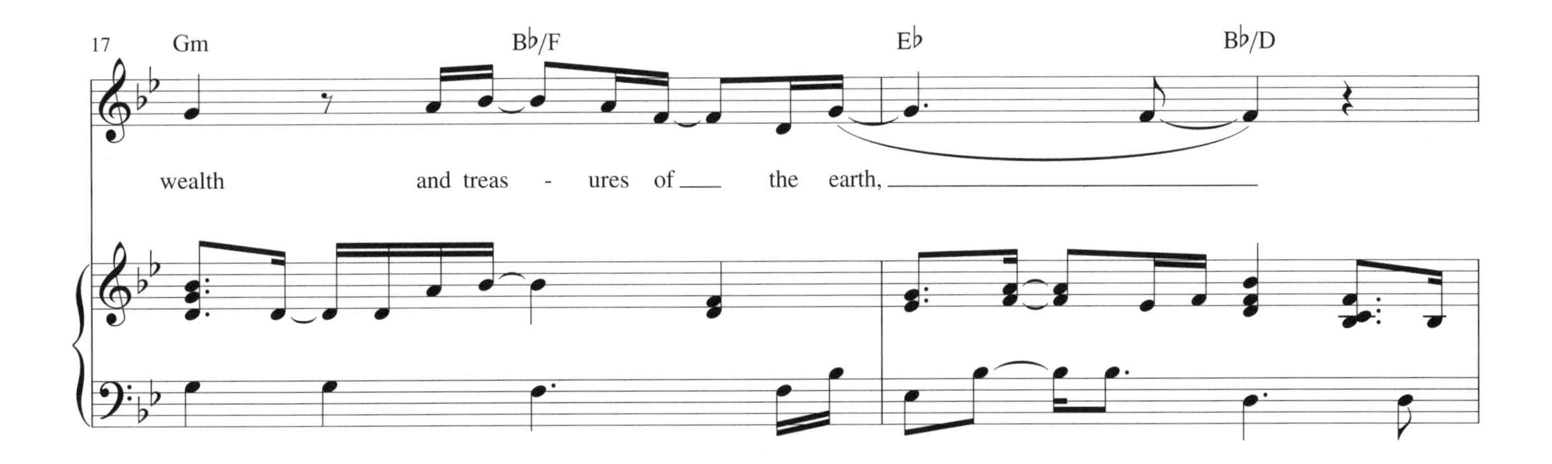
17
Gm
B♭/F
E♭
B♭/D
wealth and treas - ures of __ the earth, __

19
Cm7
D7
there's no way to meas - ure what You're worth.

21
B♭
E♭/B♭
F
B♭
Cru - ci - fied, laid be - hind a stone, You

23
E♭/B♭
F
B♭
lived to die, re - ject ed and a - lone. Like a rose

25
Gm
B♭/F
E♭
B♭/D
tram - pled on the ground, You took the fall

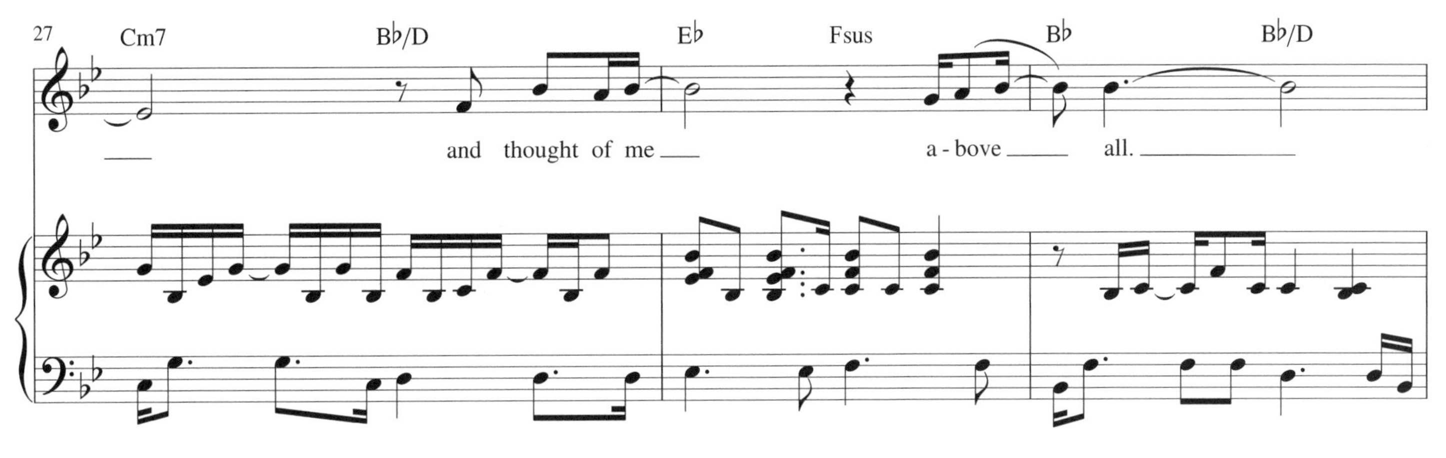
27
Cm7
B♭/D
E♭
Fsus
B♭
B♭/D
and thought of me
a-bove
all.

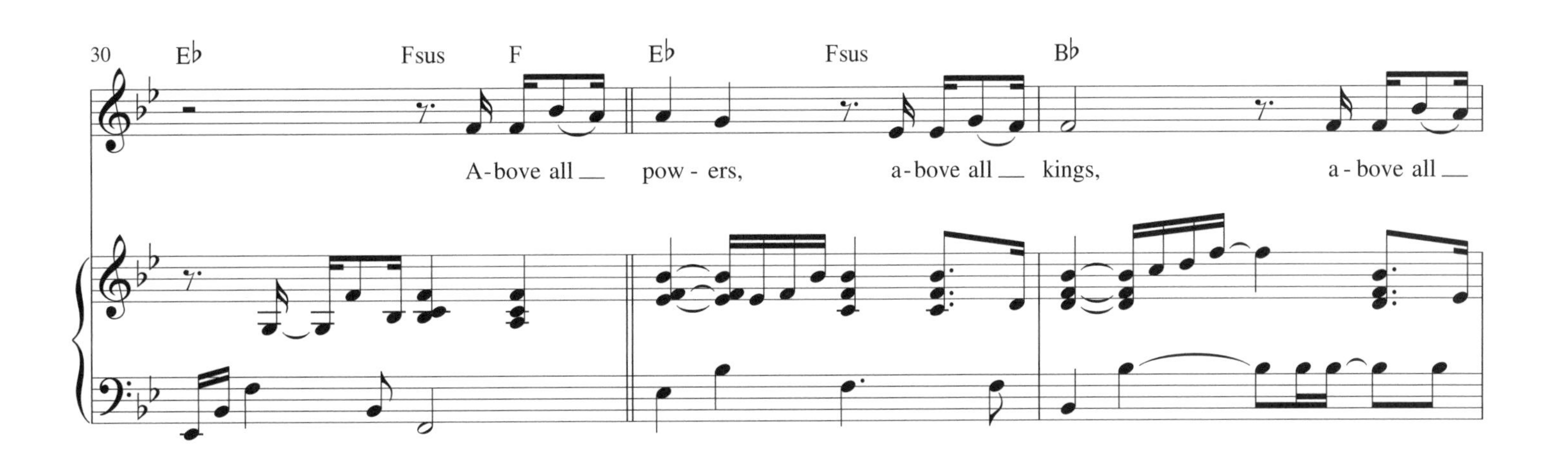
30
E♭
Fsus
F
E♭
Fsus
B♭
A-bove all
pow-ers,
a-bove all
kings,
a-bove all

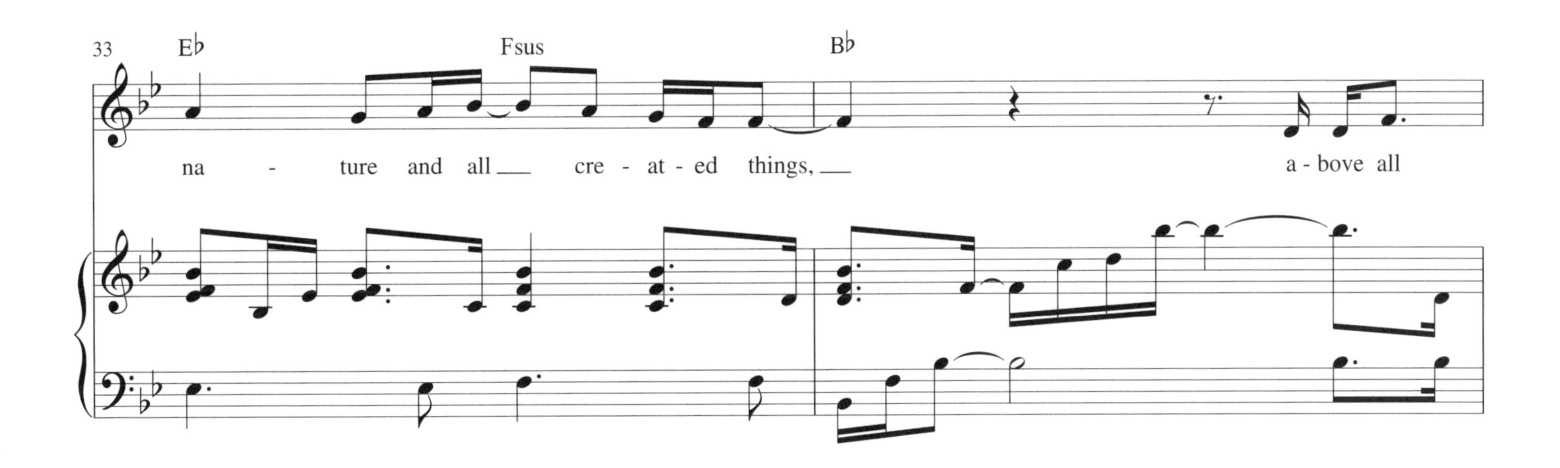
33
E♭
Fsus
B♭
na - ture and all cre - at - ed things,
a-bove all

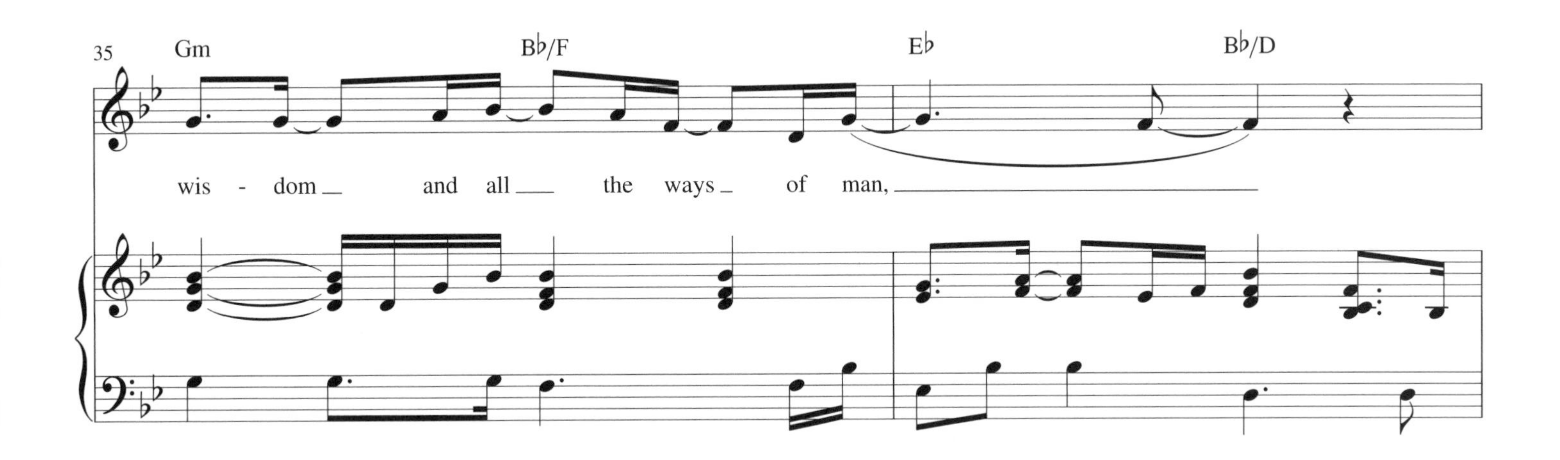
35
Gm
B♭/F
E♭
B♭/D
wis - dom and all the ways of man,

37
Cm7
Fsus
F
You were here before the world be-gan.
A-bove all

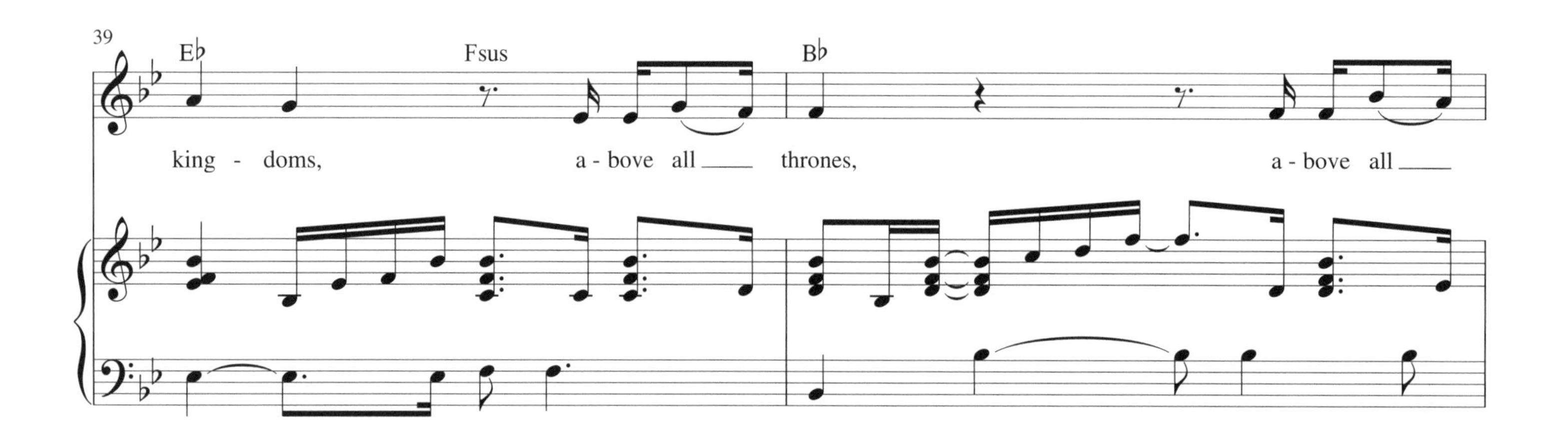
39
E♭
Fsus
B♭
king - doms,
a - bove all
thrones,
a - bove all

41
E♭
Fsus
B♭
won - ders the world has ev - er known,
a - bove all

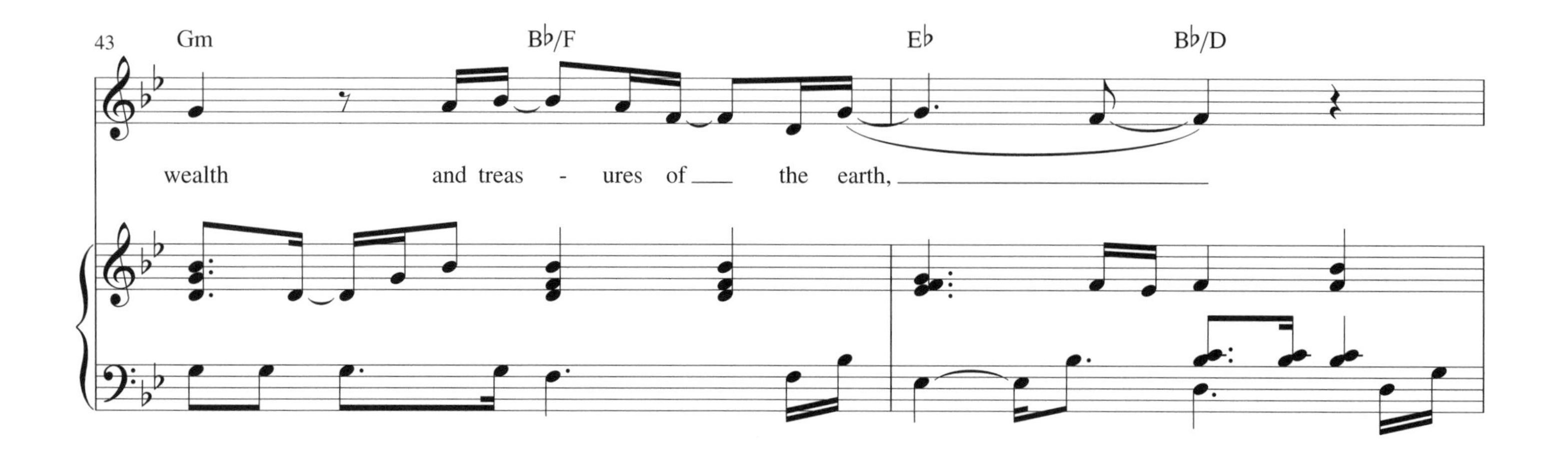
43
Gm
B♭/F
E♭
B♭/D
wealth and treas - ures of the earth,

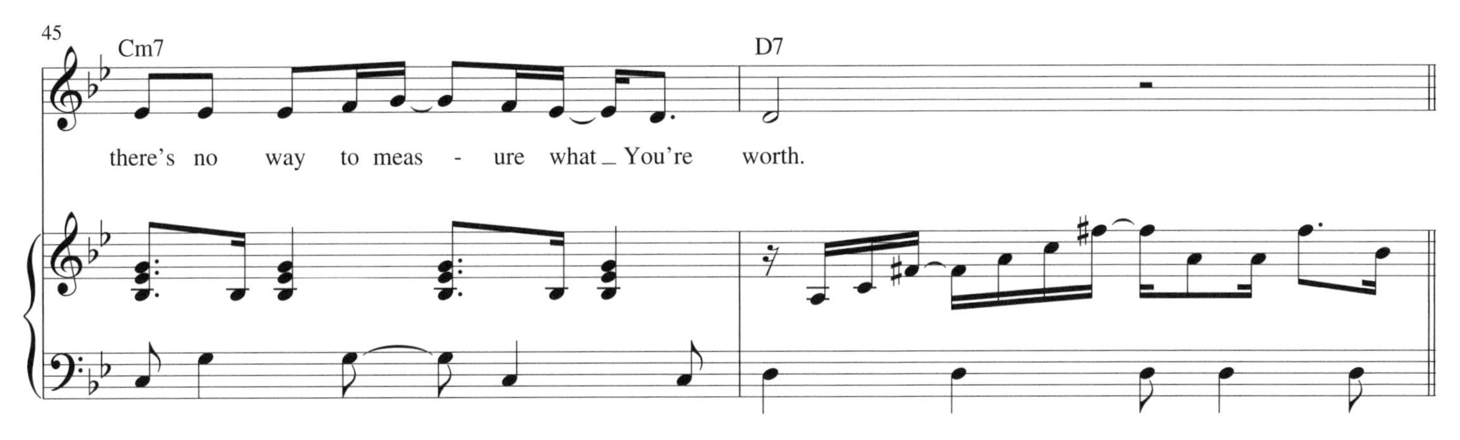
45
Cm7
D7
there's no way to meas - ure what _ You're worth.

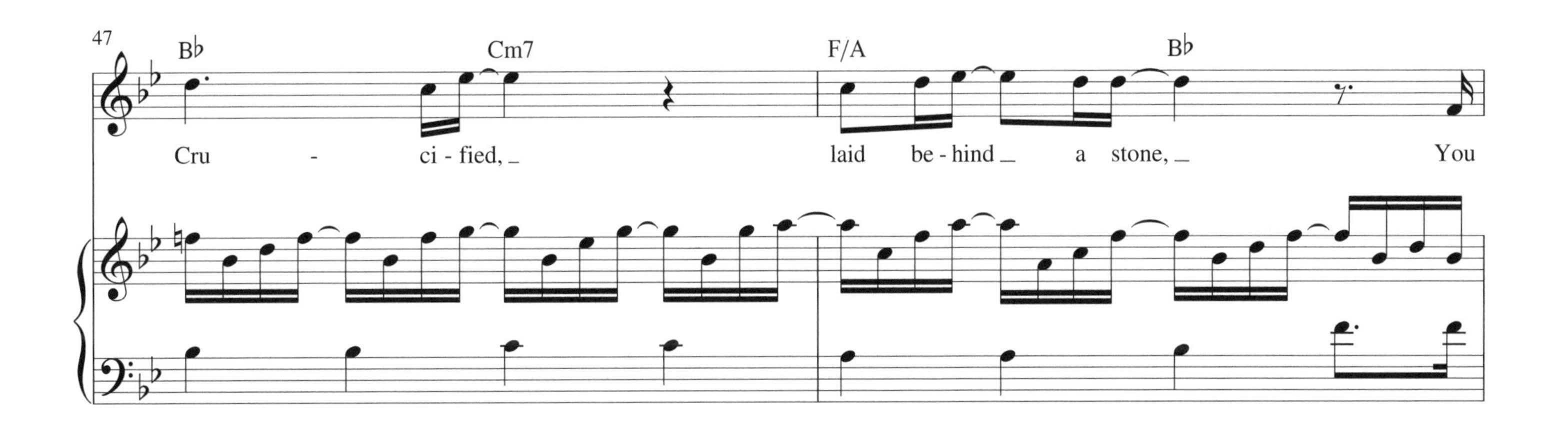
47
B♭
Cm7
F/A
B♭
Cru - ci - fied, _ laid be - hind _ a stone, _ You

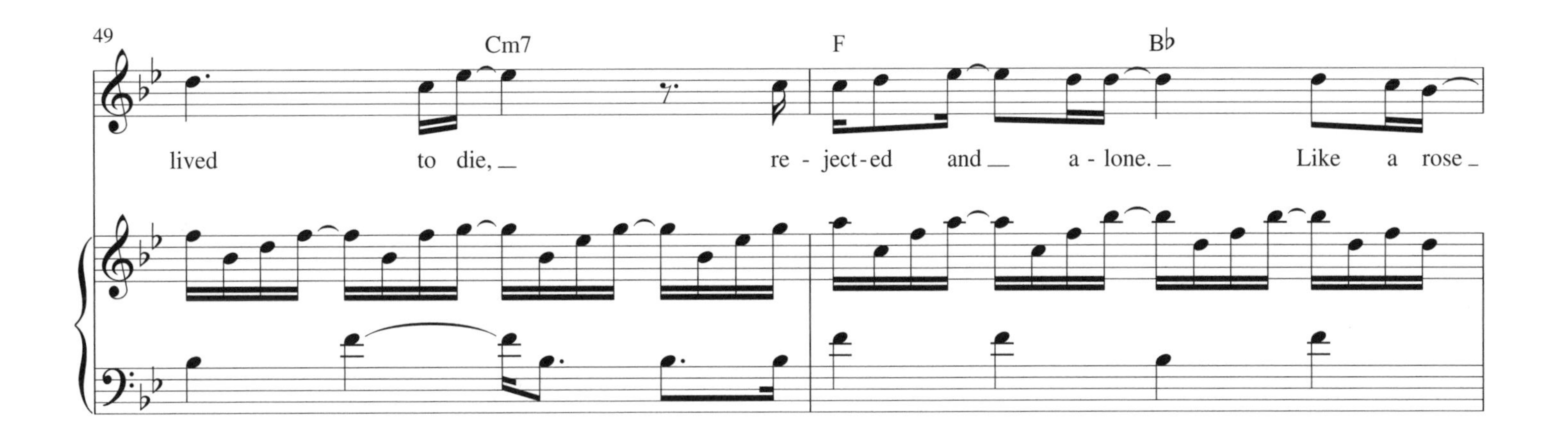
49
Cm7
F
B♭
lived to die, _ re - ject - ed and _ a - lone. _ Like a rose _

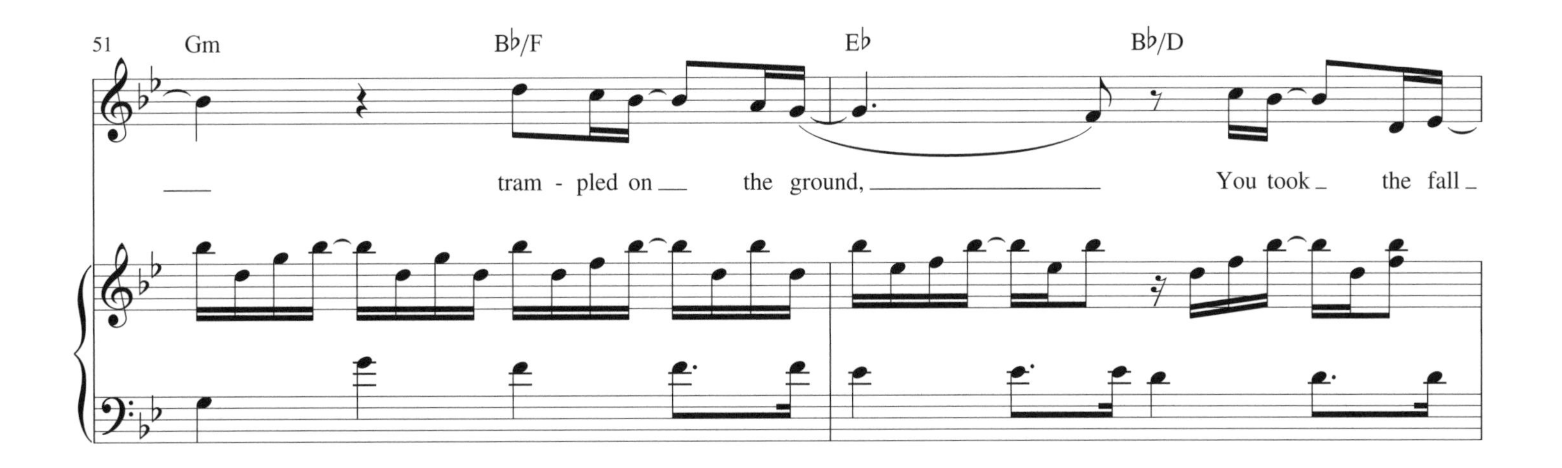
51
Gm
B♭/F
E♭
B♭/D
tram - pled on _ the ground, You took _ the fall _

53
Cm7
B♭/D
E♭
Fsus
B♭
E♭/G F/A
and thought of me a-bove all.

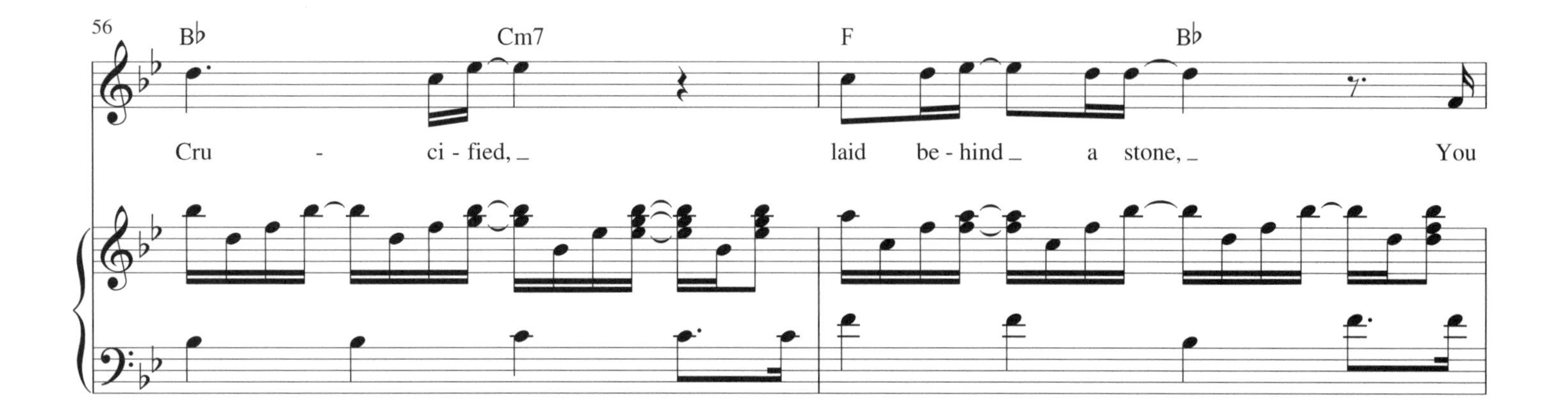
56
B♭
Cm7
F
B♭
Cru - ci-fied, laid be-hind a stone, You

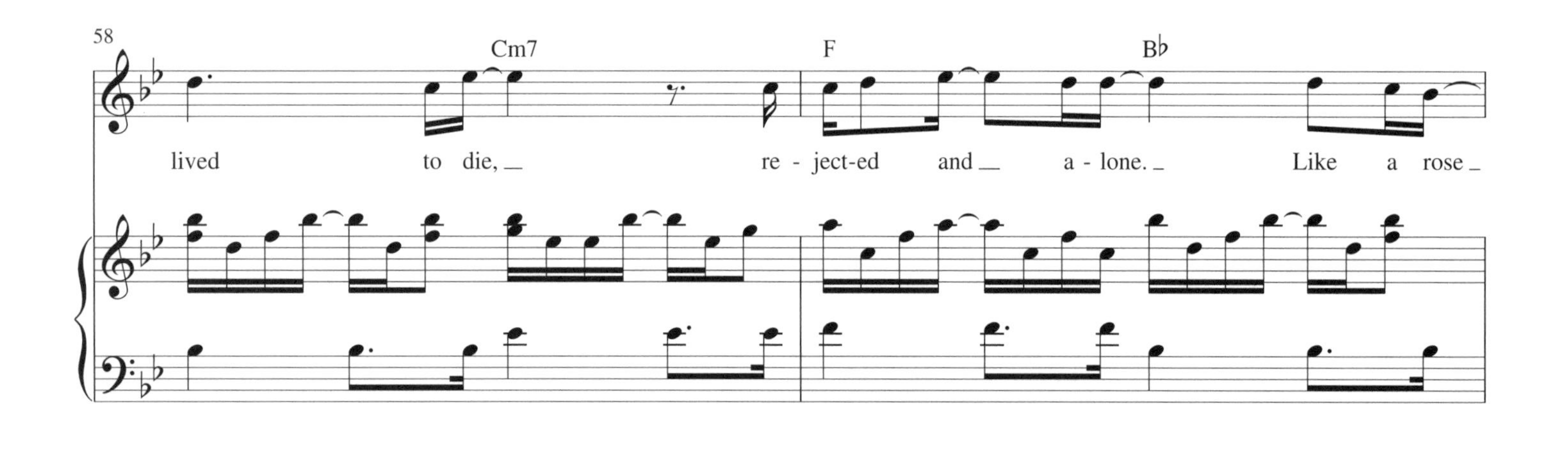
58
Cm7
F
B♭
lived to die, re-ject-ed and a-lone. Like a rose

60
Gm
B♭/F
E♭
B♭/D
tram-pled on the ground, You took the fall

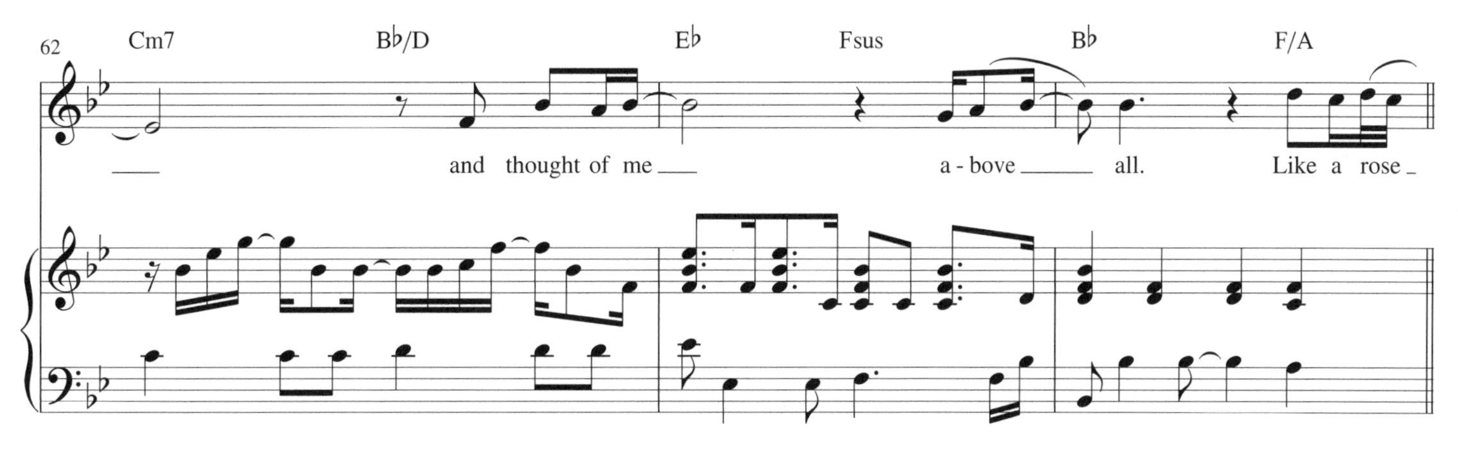
62
Cm7 B♭/D E♭ Fsus B♭ F/A
and thought of me a - bove all. Like a rose

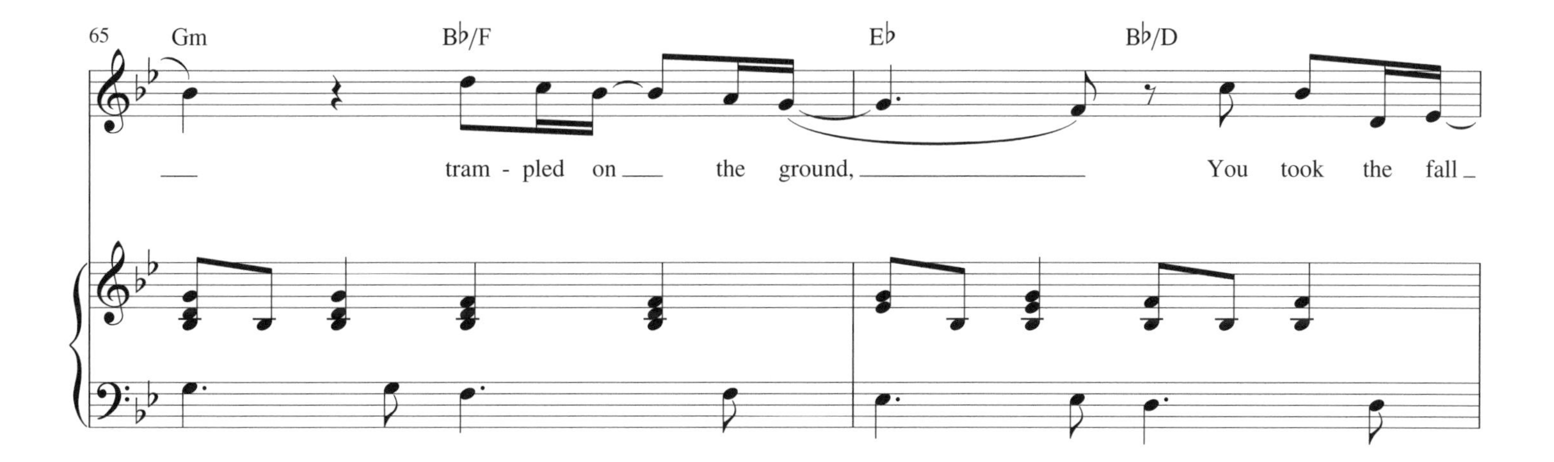
65
Gm B♭/F E♭ B♭/D
tram - pled on the ground, You took the fall

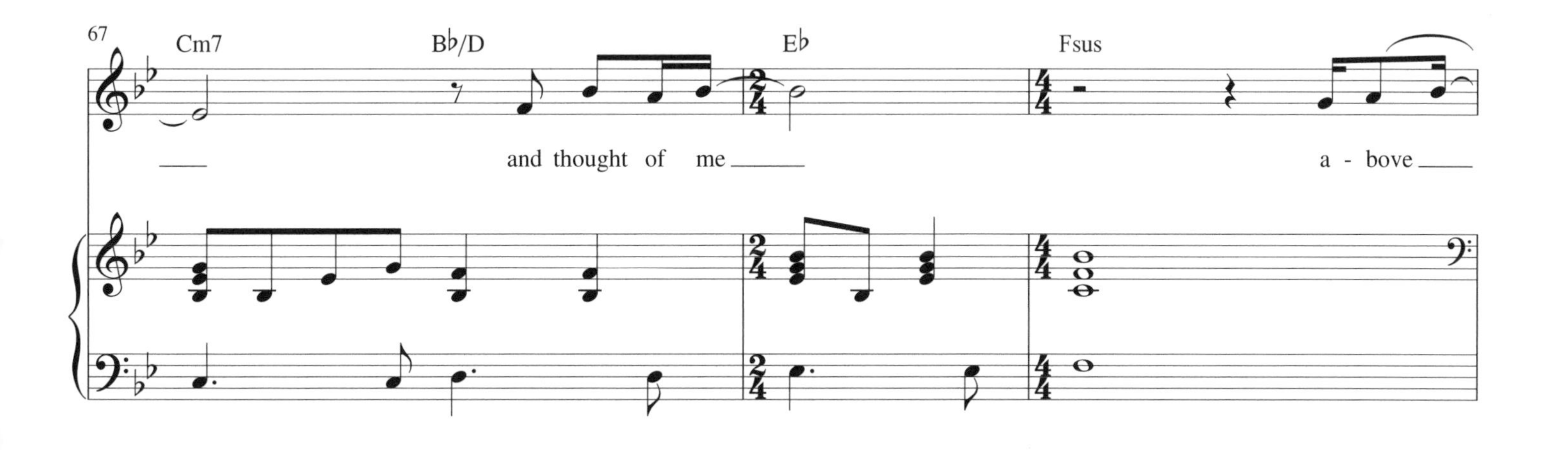
67
Cm7 B♭/D E♭ Fsus
and thought of me a - bove

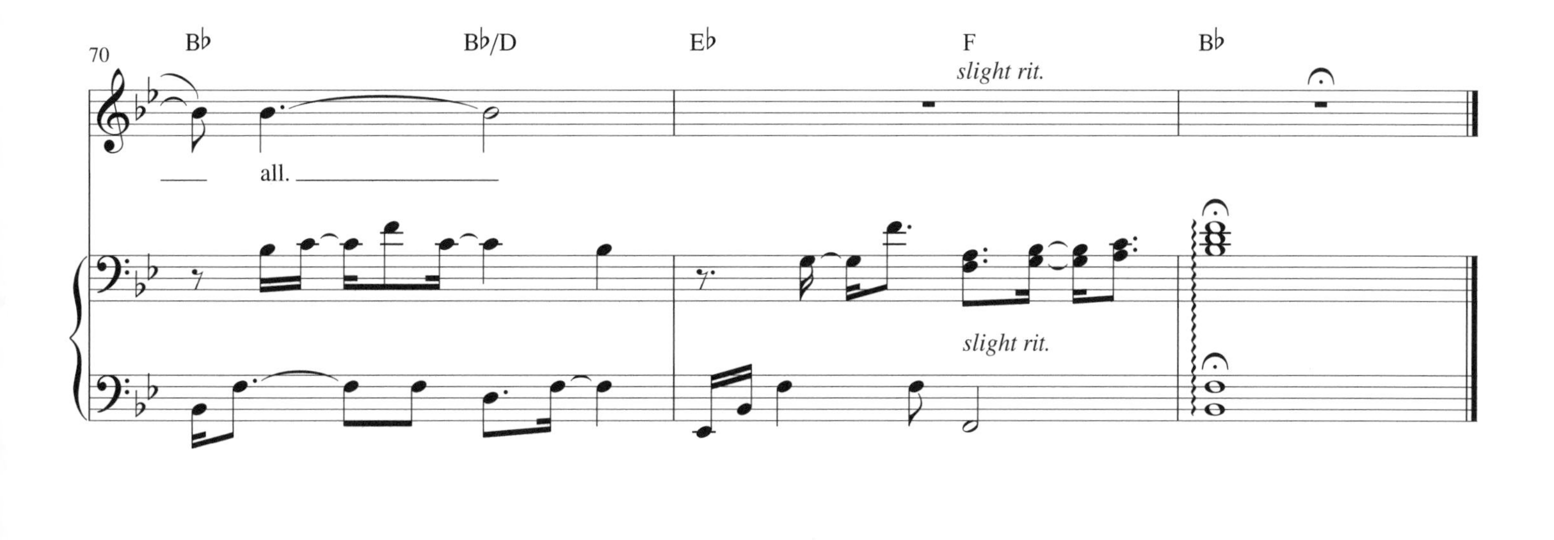
70
B♭ B♭/D E♭ F B♭
slight rit.
all.
slight rit.

This page has been left blank to facilitate page turns.

Amazing Grace
(My Chains Are Gone)

Words by JOHN NEWTON
Traditional American Melody
Additional Words and Music by CHRIS TOMLIN
and LOUIE GIGLIO

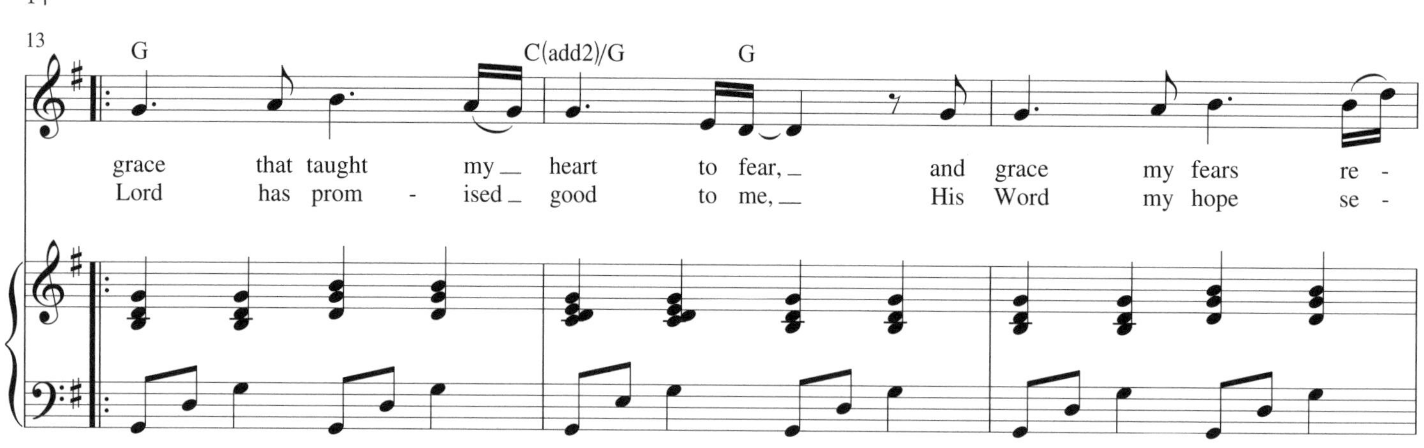
13
G
C(add2)/G
G
grace that taught my heart to fear, and grace my fears re -
Lord has prom - ised good to me, His Word my hope se -

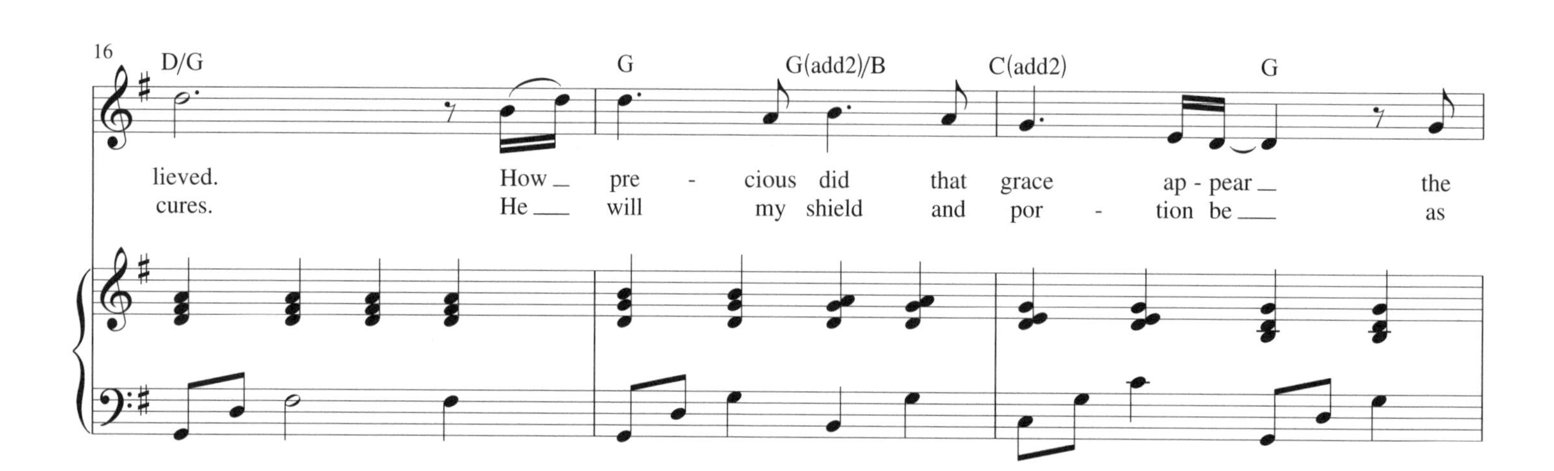
16
D/G
G
G(add2)/B
C(add2)
G
lieved. How pre - cious did that grace ap - pear the
cures. He will my shield and por - tion be as

19
D/G
G
C/G
G
C
hour I first be - lieved.
long as life en - dures.
My chains are gone, I've been set
mf

22
G/B
C
free. My God, my Sav - ior has ran - somed

24
G/D G/B C G/B
me. And like a flood, His mer - cy rains un - end - ing

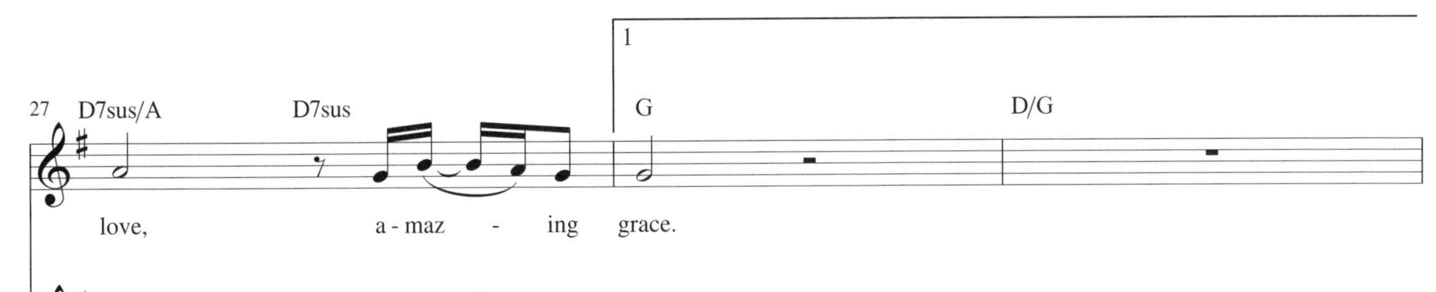
1
27
D7sus/A D7sus G D/G
love, a - maz - ing grace.
mp

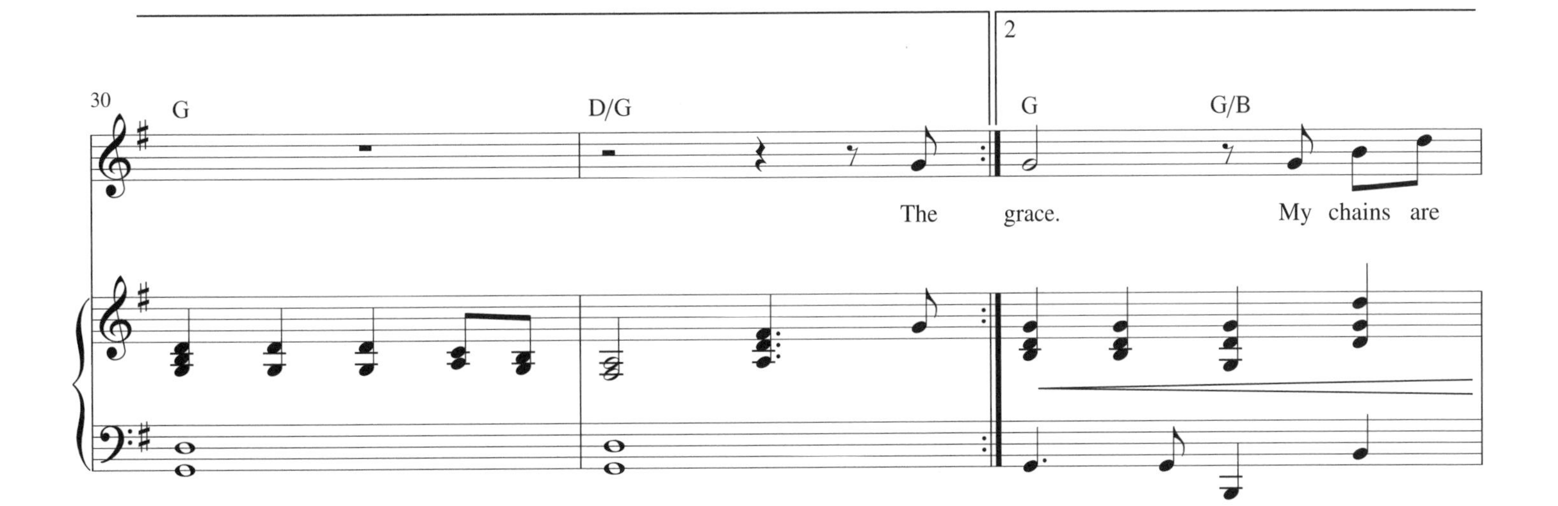
2
30
G D/G G G/B
The grace. My chains are

33
C G/B
gone, I've been set free. My God, my

35
C/E
G/D
Sav - ior has ran - somed me. And like a

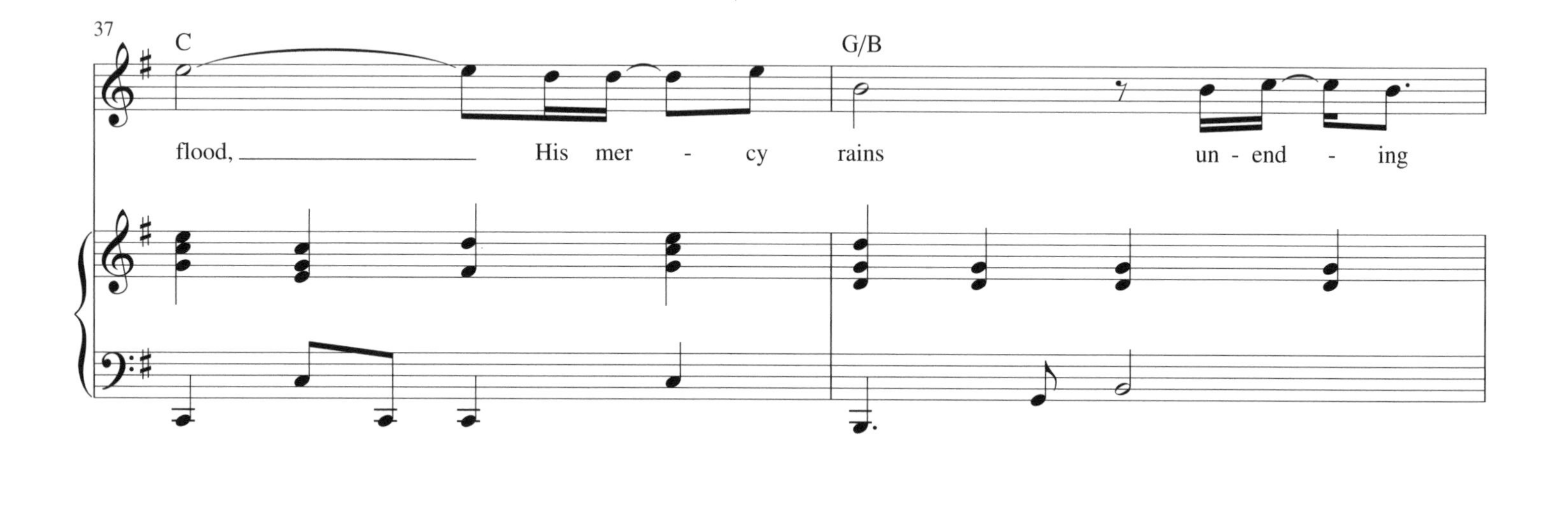
37
C
G/B
flood, His mer - cy rains un - end - ing

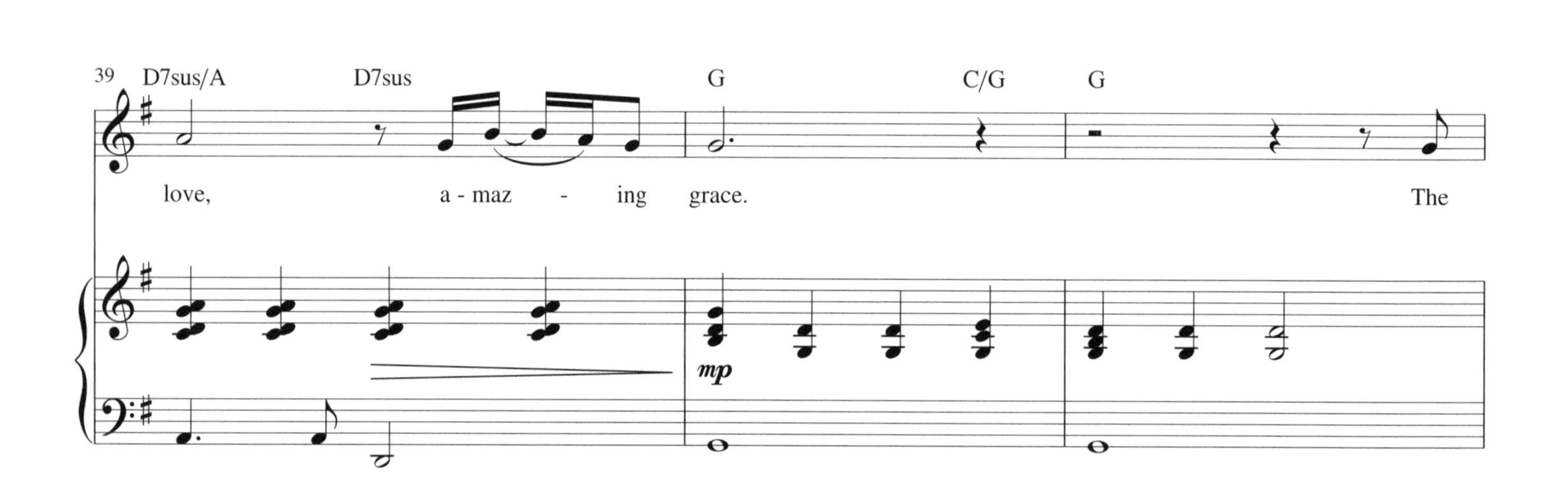
39
D7sus/A
D7sus
G
C/G
G
love, a - maz - ing grace. The
mp

42
G(add2)
Gsus
G
earth shall soon dis - solve like snow, the sun for - bear to

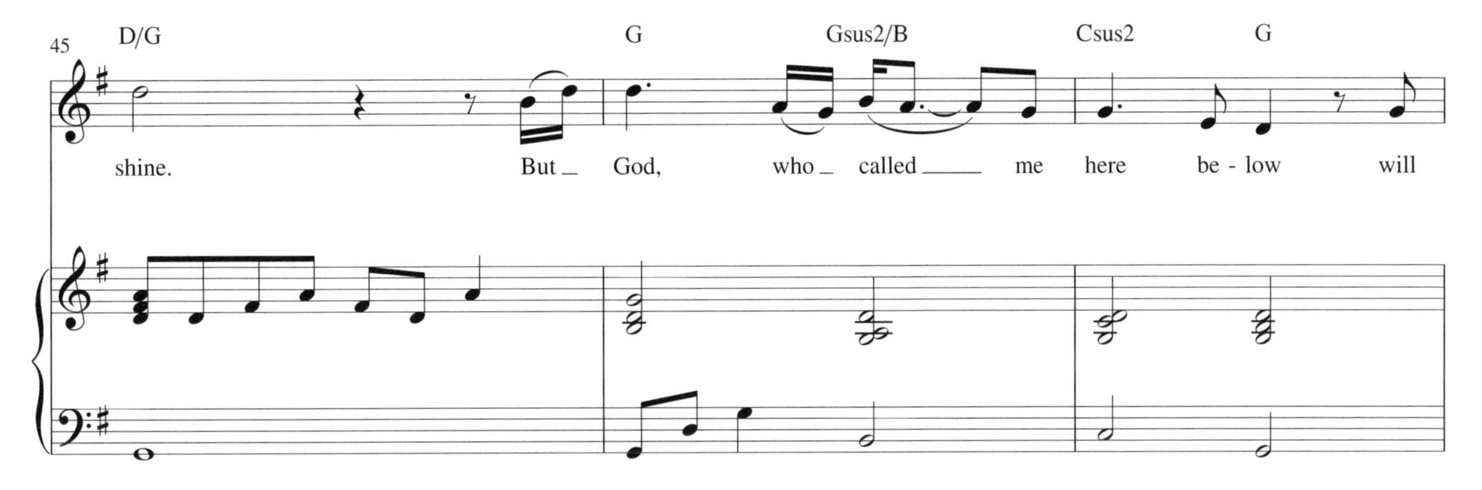
45
D/G
G
Gsus2/B
Csus2
G
shine.
But _
God,
who _
called ____
me
here
be - low
will

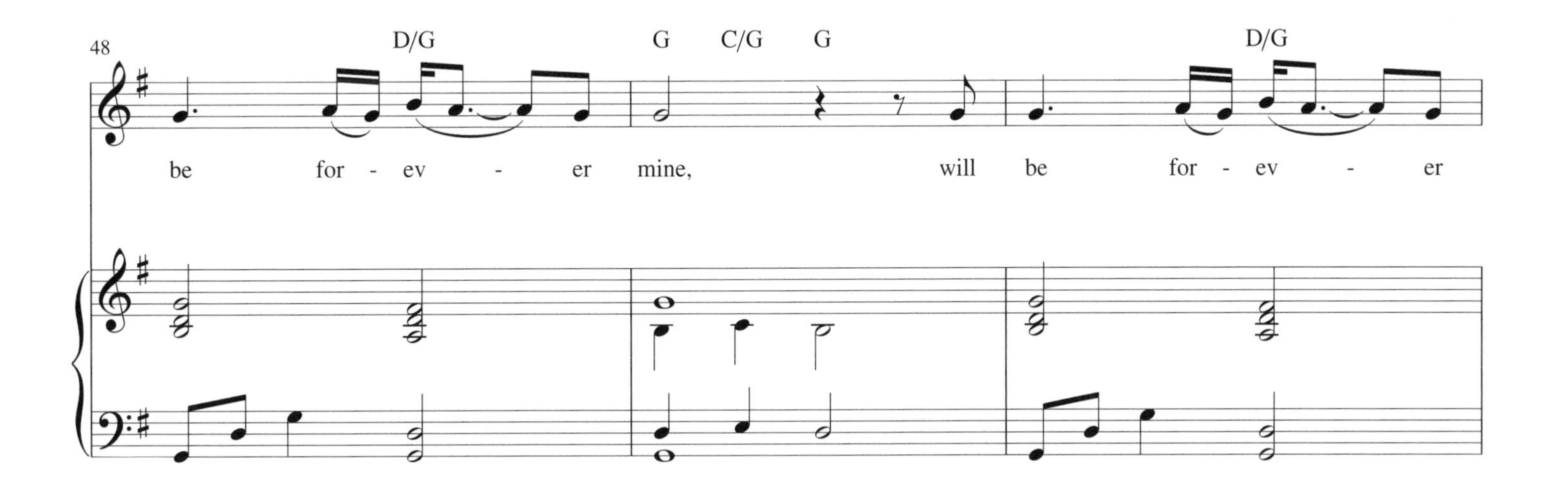
48
D/G
G
C/G
G
D/G
be
for -
ev
-
er
mine,
will
be
for -
ev
-
er

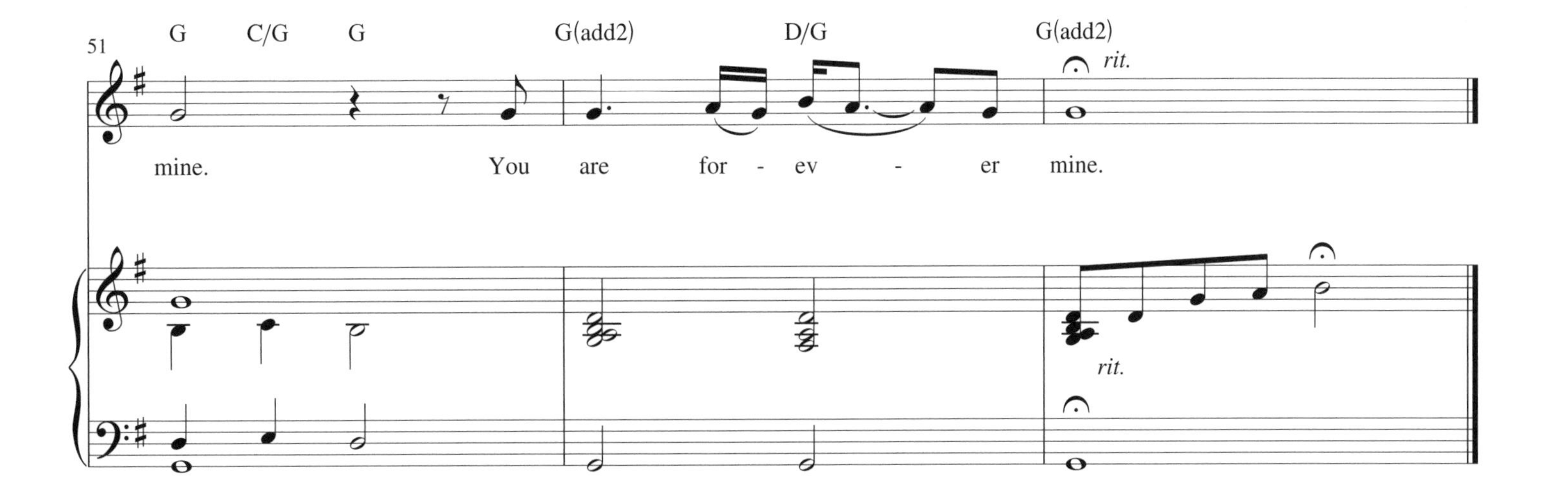
51
G
C/G
G
G(add2)
D/G
G(add2)
rit.
mine.
You
are
for -
ev
-
er
mine.
rit.

Holy Ground

Words and Music by
GERON DAVIS

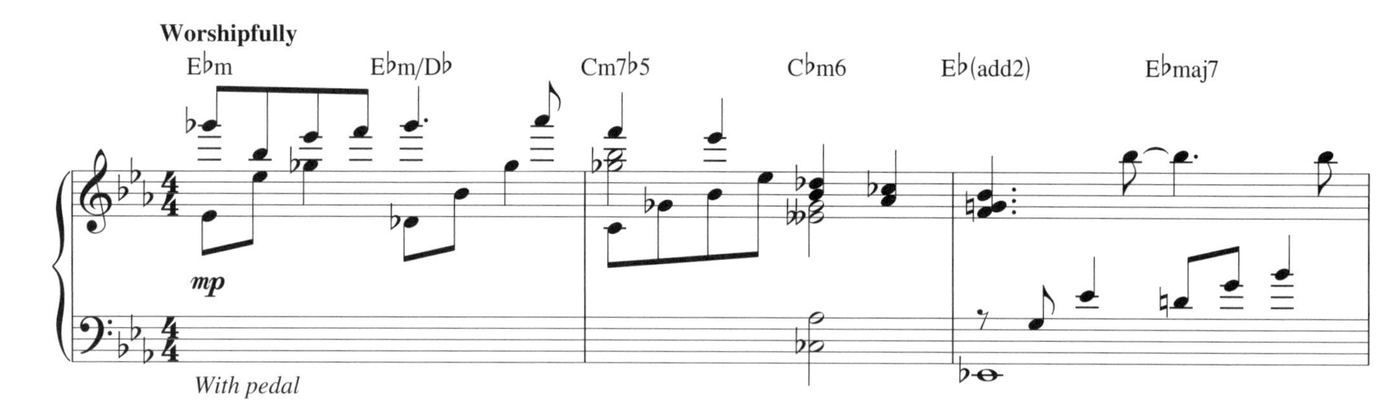

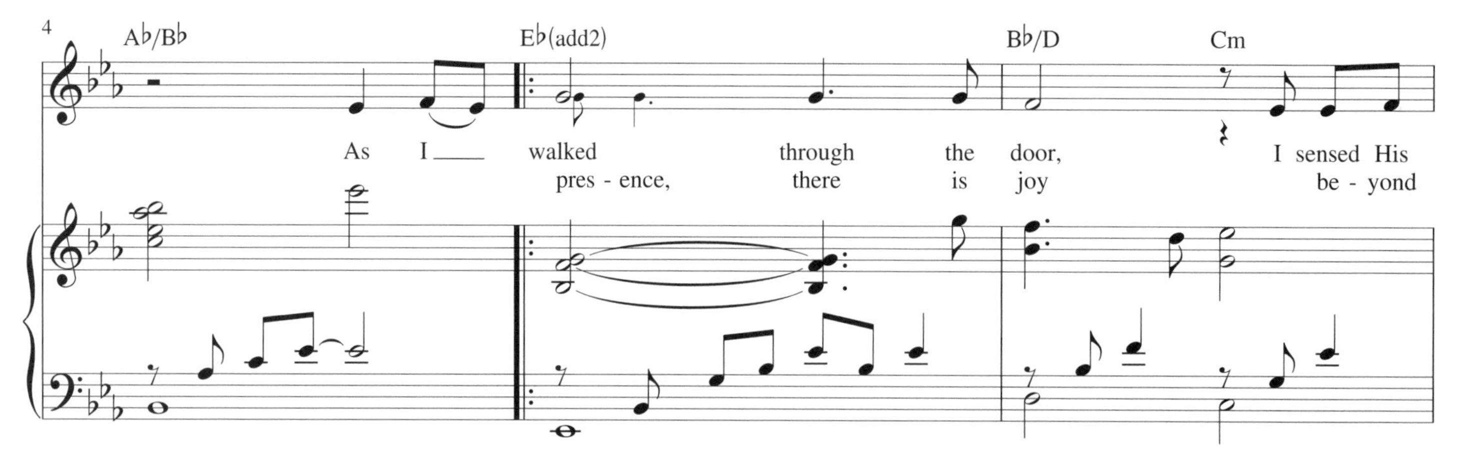

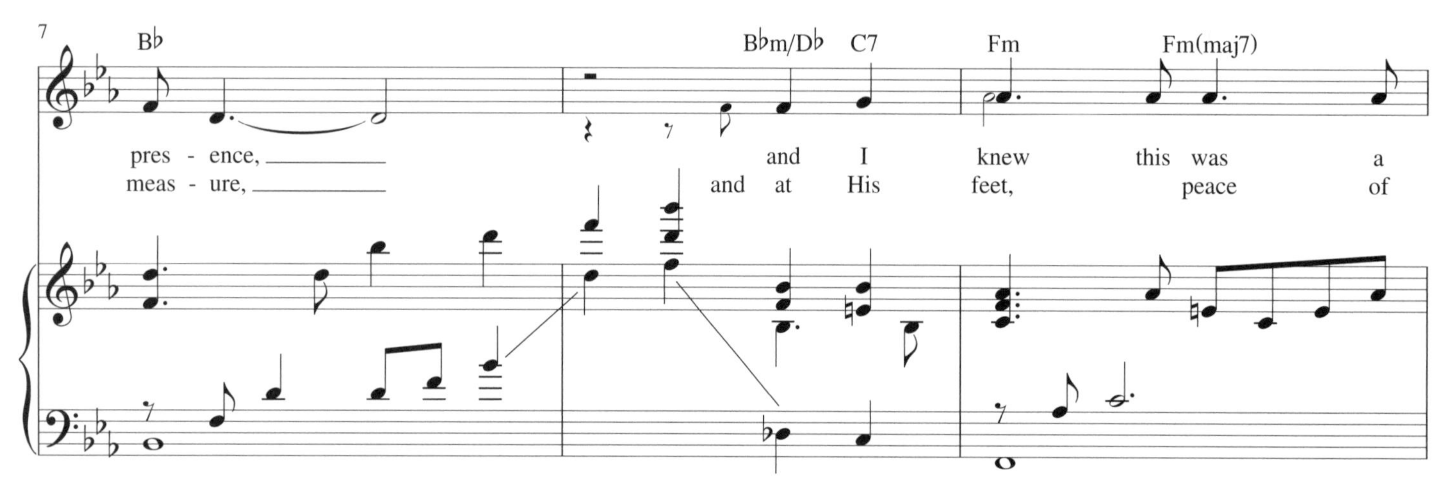

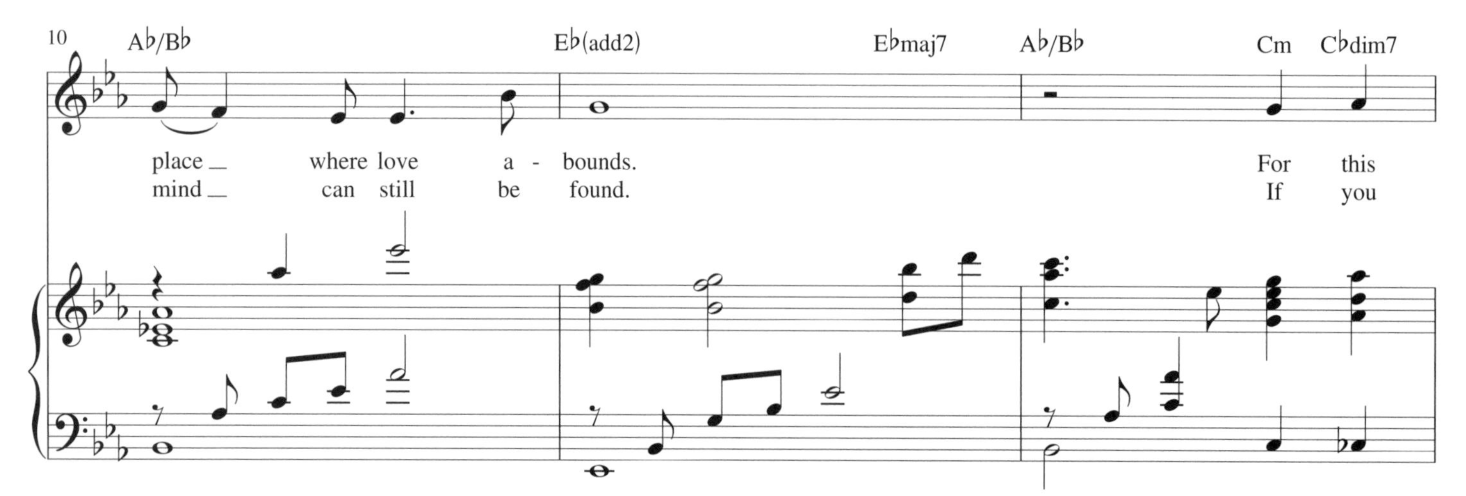

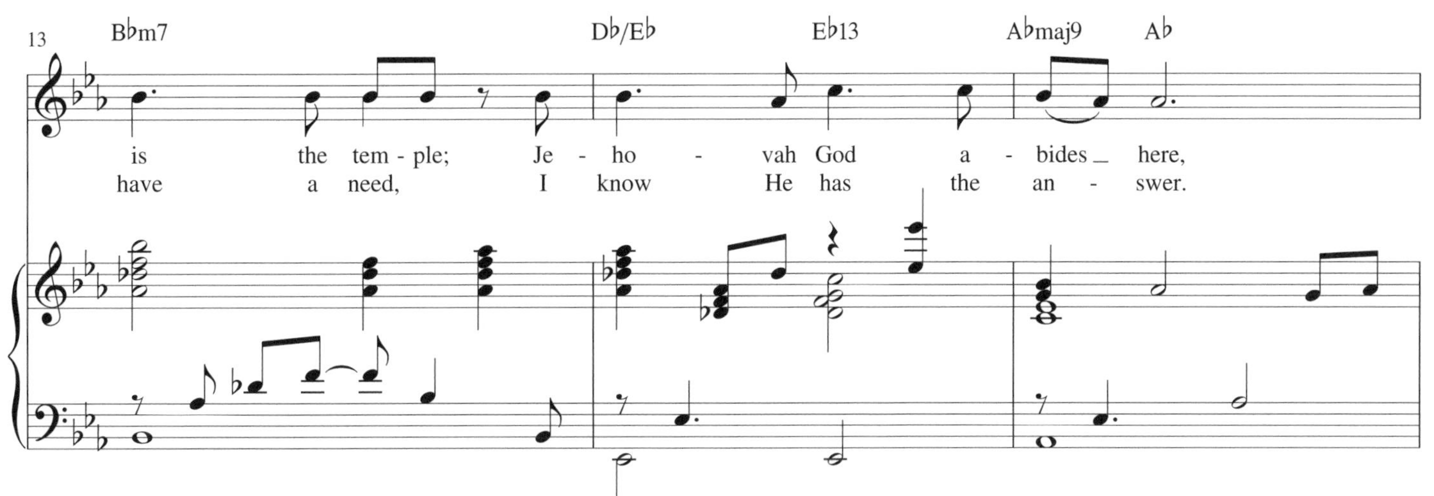
13
B♭m7
D♭/E♭
E♭13
A♭maj9
A♭
is the tem - ple; Je - ho - vah God a - bides _ here,
have a need, I know He has the an - swer.

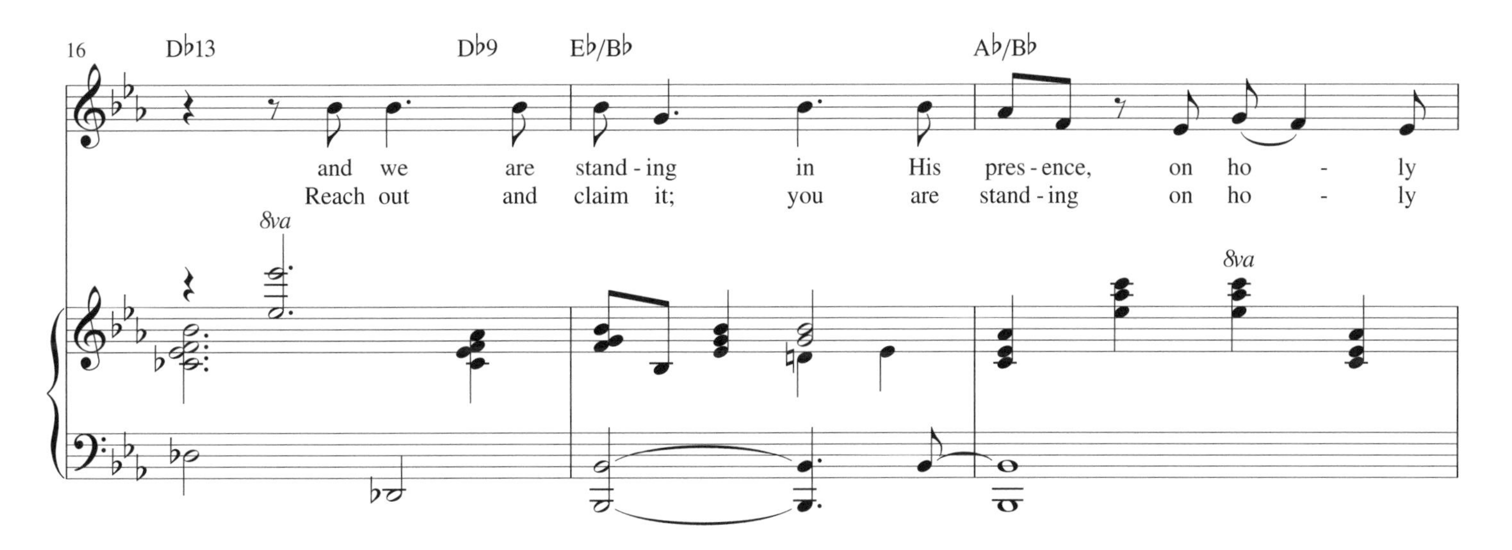
16
D♭13
D♭9
E♭/B♭
A♭/B♭
and we are stand - ing in His pres - ence, on ho - ly
Reach out and claim it; you are stand - ing on ho - ly
8va
8va

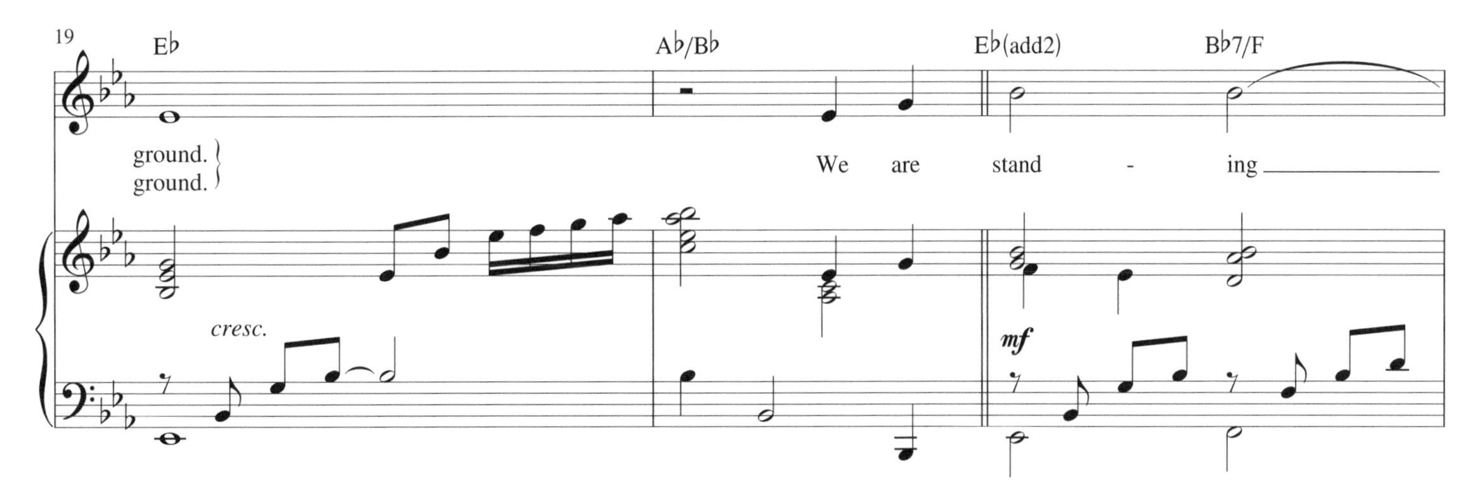
19
E♭
A♭/B♭
E♭(add2)
B♭7/F
ground.
ground.
We are stand - ing
cresc.
mf

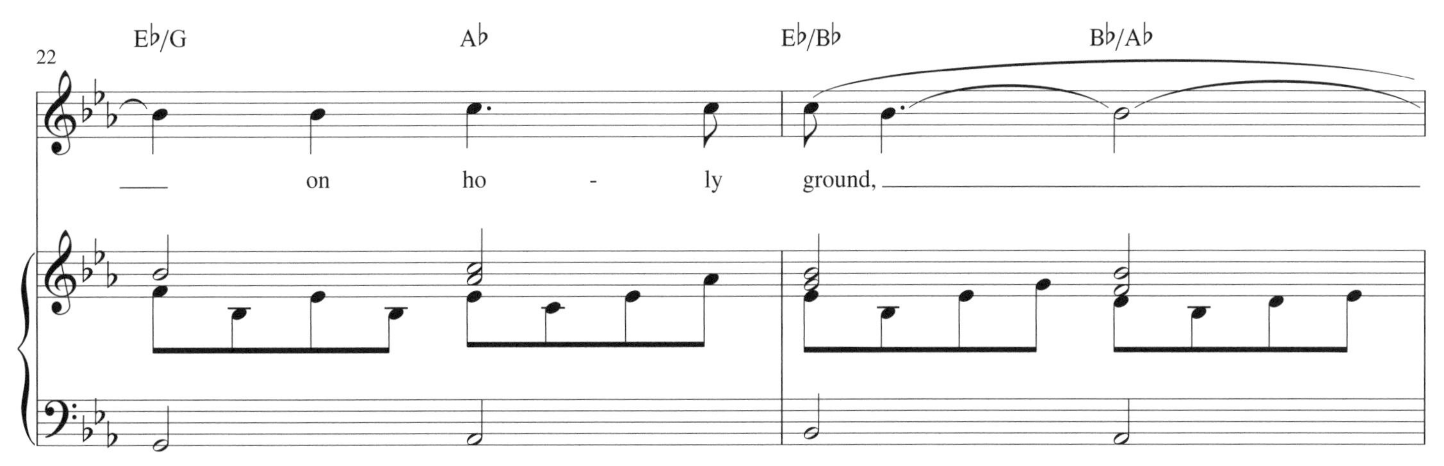
22
E♭/G
A♭
E♭/B♭
B♭/A♭
on ho - ly ground,

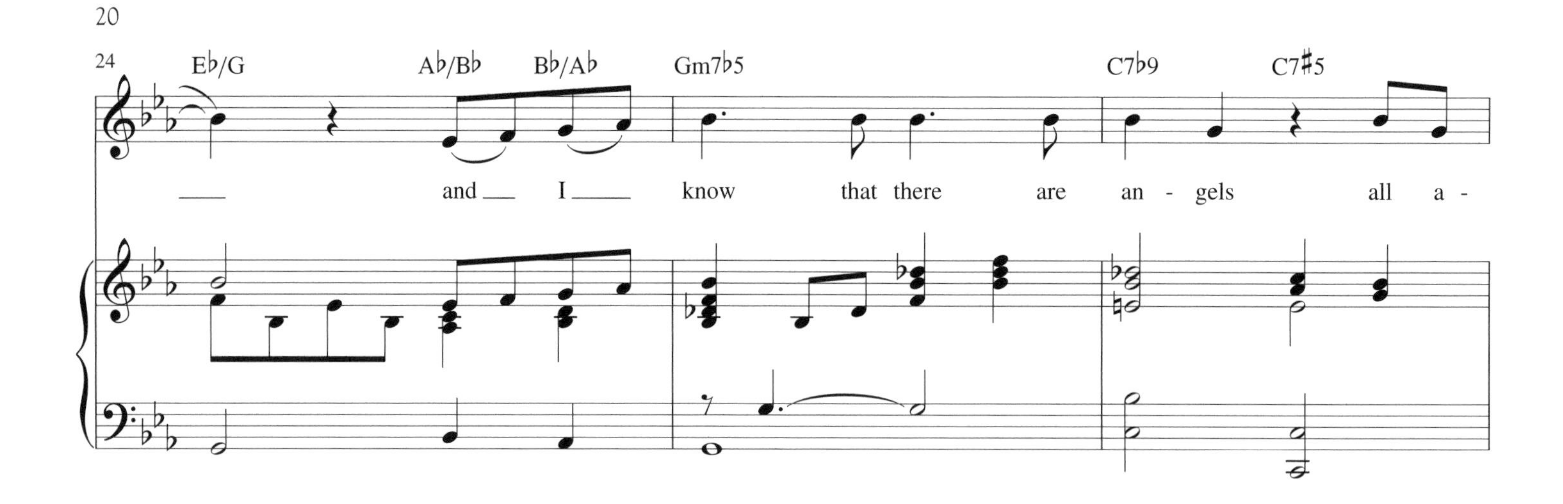
24
E♭/G
A♭/B♭
B♭/A♭
Gm7♭5
C7♭9
C7♯5
and I know that there are an - gels all a -

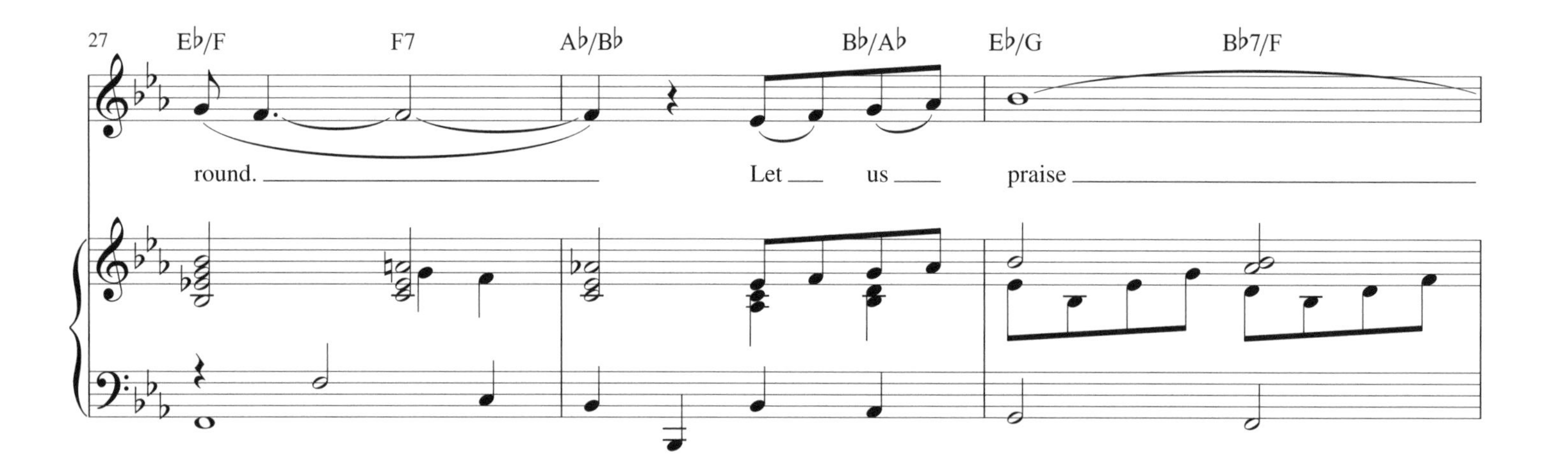
27
E♭/F
F7
A♭/B♭
B♭/A♭
E♭/G
B♭7/F
round. Let us praise

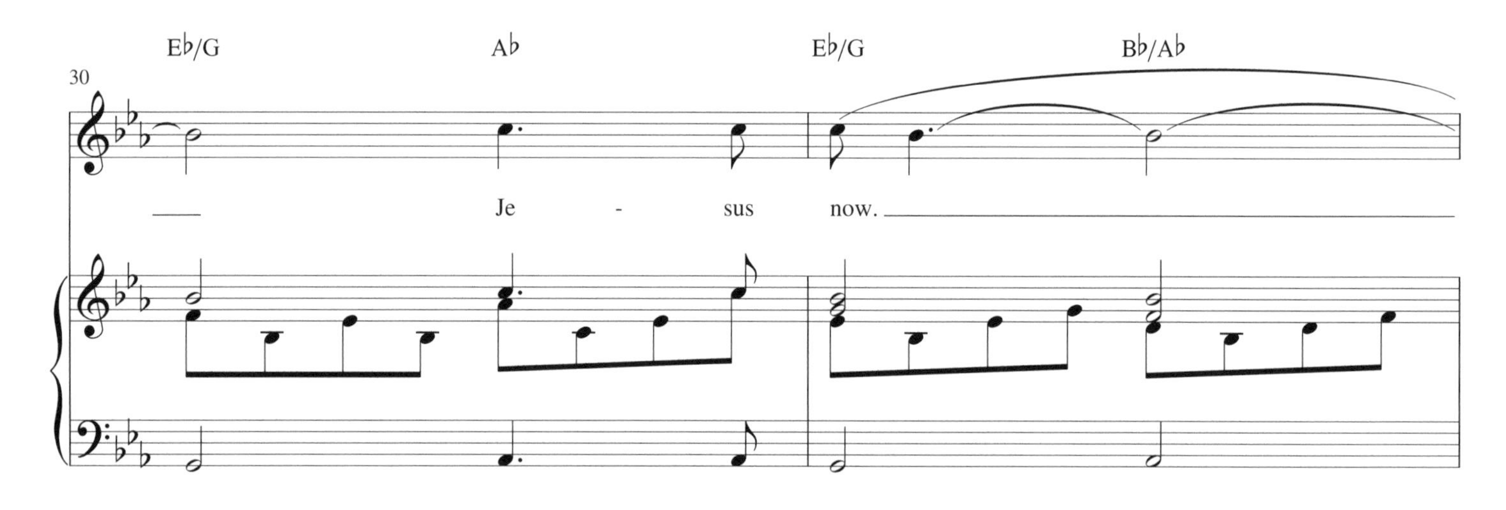
30
E♭/G
A♭
E♭/G
B♭/A♭
Je - sus now.

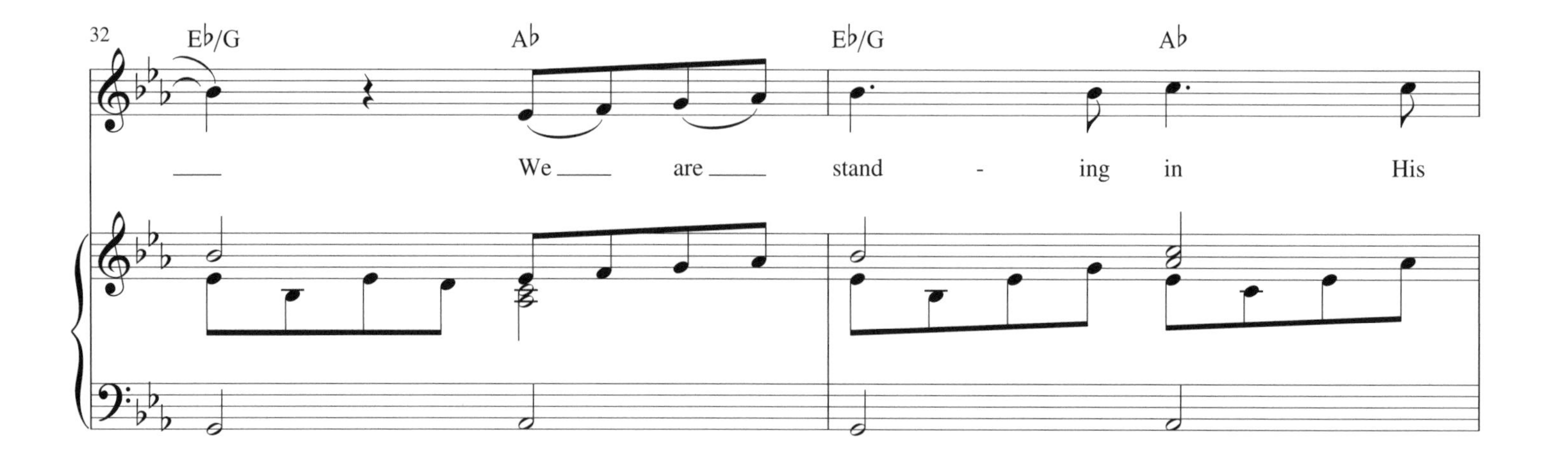
32
E♭/G
A♭
E♭/G
A♭
We are stand - ing in His

34
Eb/Bb
Ab/Bb
1
Eb
pres-ence, on ho - ly ground.
dim.
mp

37
Ebm
Ebm/Db
Cm7b5
Cbm6
Eb(add2)
Ebmaj7

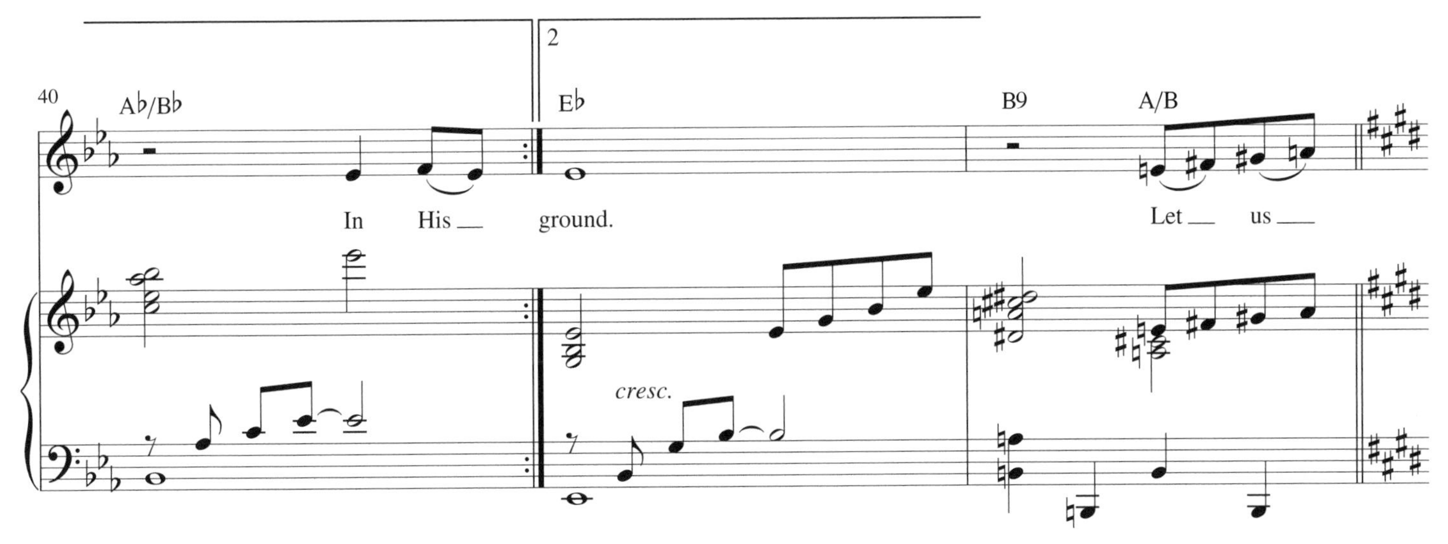
40
Ab/Bb
2
Eb
B9
A/B
In His ground.
Let us
cresc.

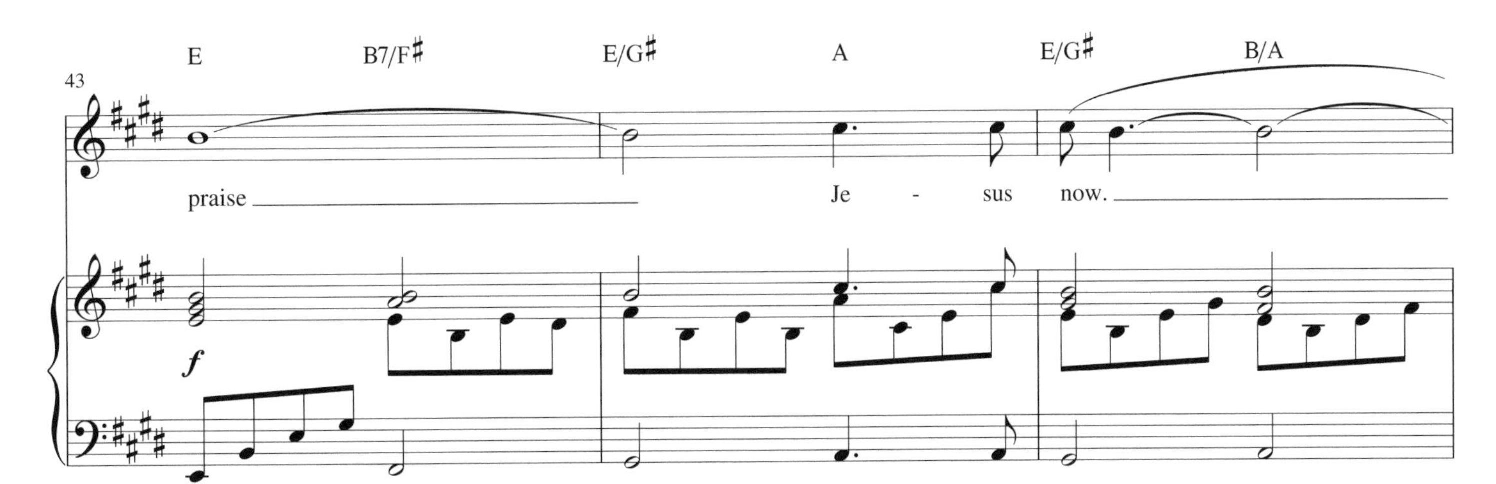
43
E
B7/F#
E/G#
A
E/G#
B/A
praise Je - sus now.
f

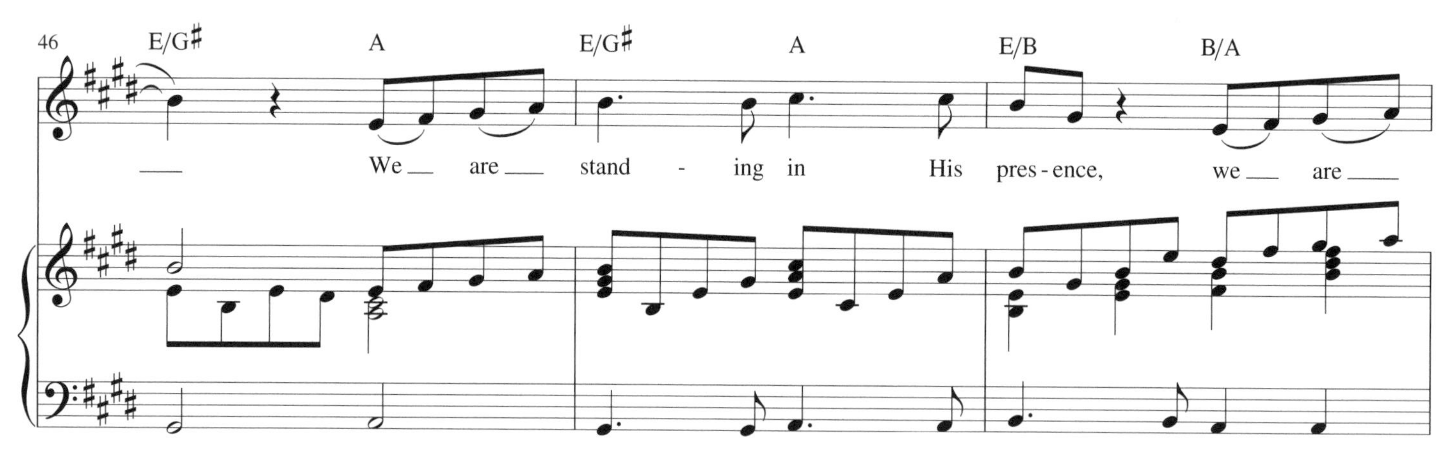
46
E/G♯
A
E/G♯
A
E/B
B/A
We are stand - ing in His pres - ence, we are

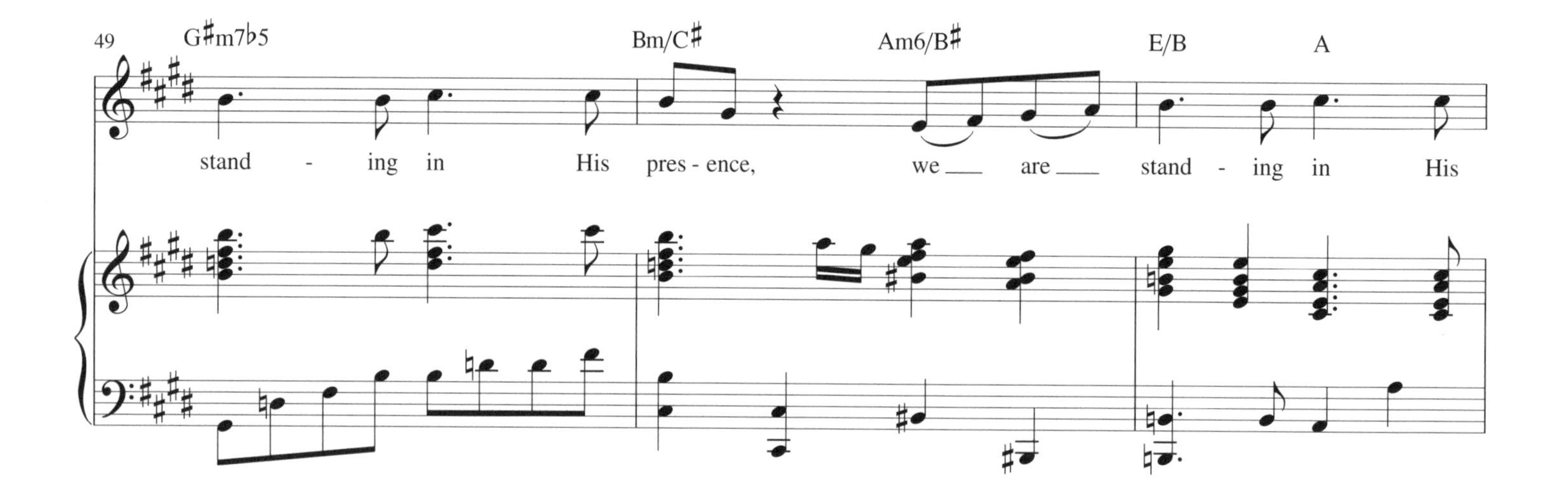
49
G♯m7♭5
Bm/C♯
Am6/B♯
E/B
A
stand - ing in His pres - ence, we are stand - ing in His

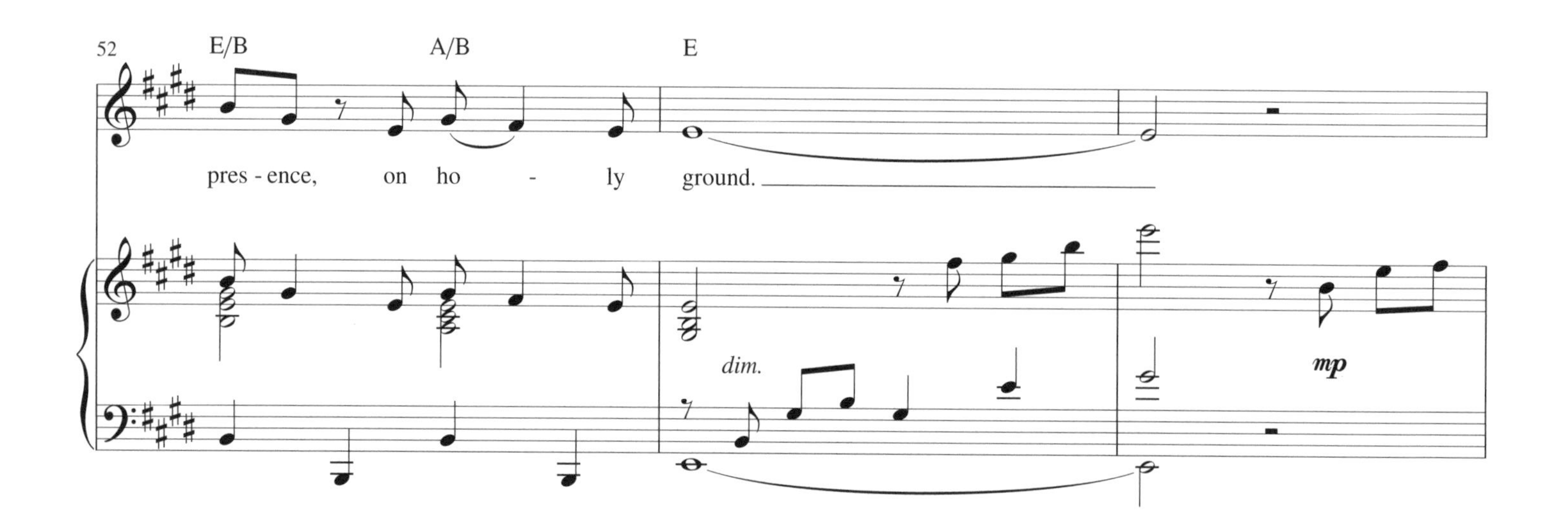
52
E/B
A/B
E
pres - ence, on ho - ly ground.
dim.
mp

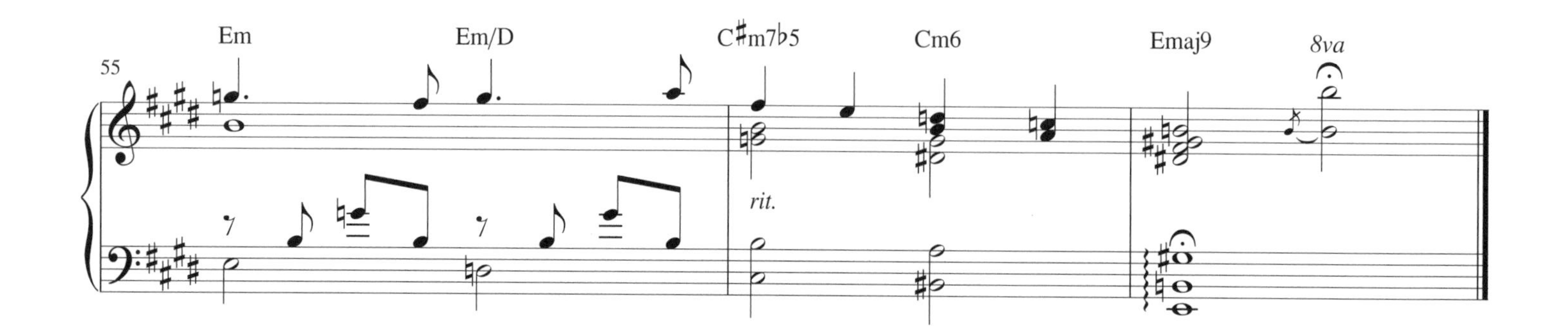
55
Em
Em/D
C♯m7♭5
Cm6
Emaj9
8va
rit.

From the Inside Out

Words and Music by
JOEL HOUSTON

9
C G Am7 Fmaj7
in Your grace. Ev - er - last - ing, Your light will shine when
ing You praise.
11
C G Am7 Fmaj7
1
C G
all else fades. Nev-er-end - ing, Your glo - ry goes be - yond all fame.

14 F(add2) C G F(add2)

17
C G
2,3
C G Fsus2
Your will a - yond all fame. In my heart and my soul,

20
C
Am7
Gsus
well, I give You con - trol.
Con - sume me from the in - side out, Lord.

To Coda
23
Fsus2
Am7
Gsus
And let jus - tice and praise
be - come my em - brace,
to love You from the

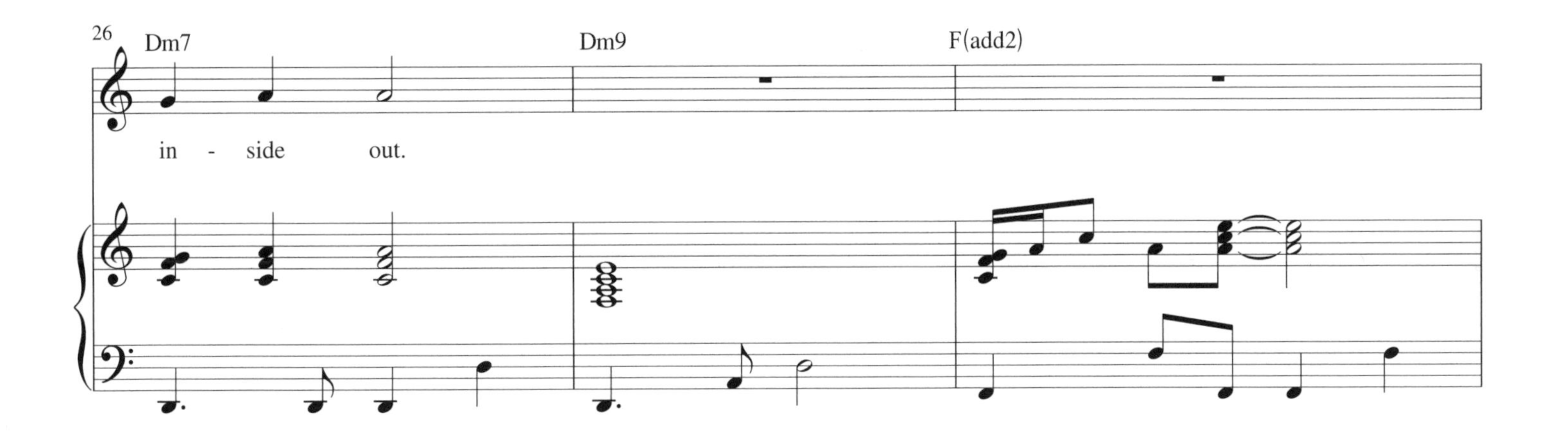
26
Dm7
Dm9
F(add2)
in - side out.

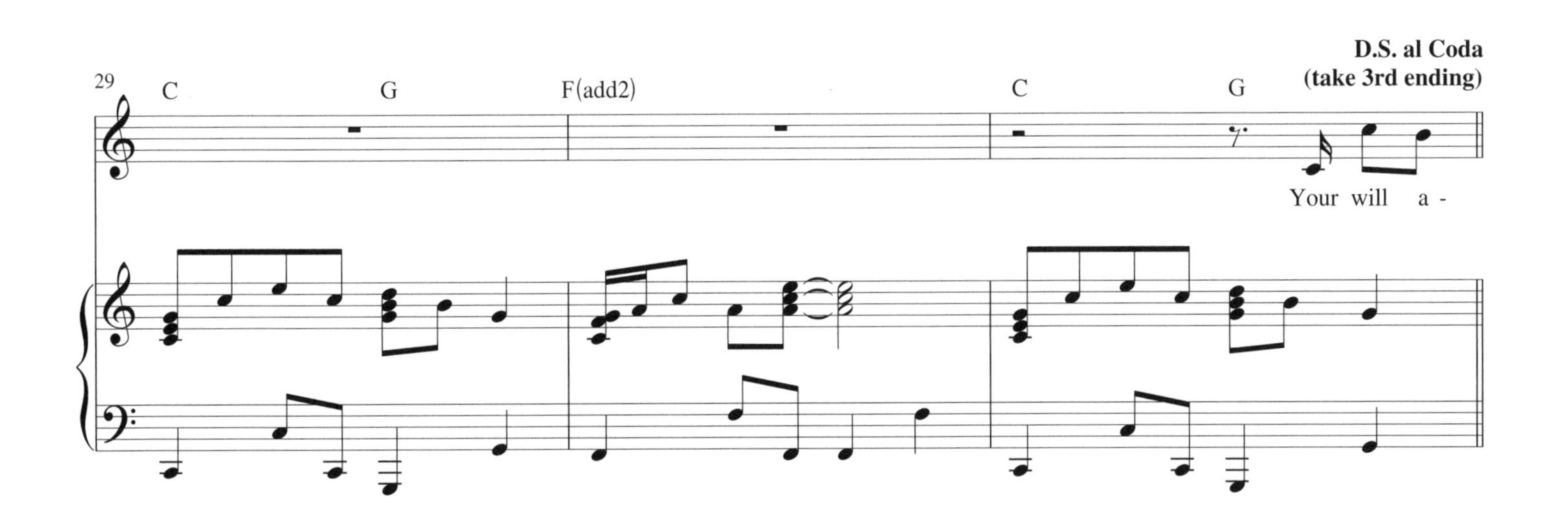
D.S. al Coda
(take 3rd ending)
29
C
G
F(add2)
C
G
Your will a -

CODA
32
Dm7
Am7
Fmaj7
C
G
in - side out. Ev - er - last - ing, Your light will shine when all else fades. Nev - er - end -
f

35
Am7
Fmaj7
C
G
C
F
- ing, Your glo - ry goes be - yond all fame. And the cry of my heart is to bring

38
G
Am7
F
G
F
G
You praise. From the in - side out, Lord, my soul cries out, Lord.

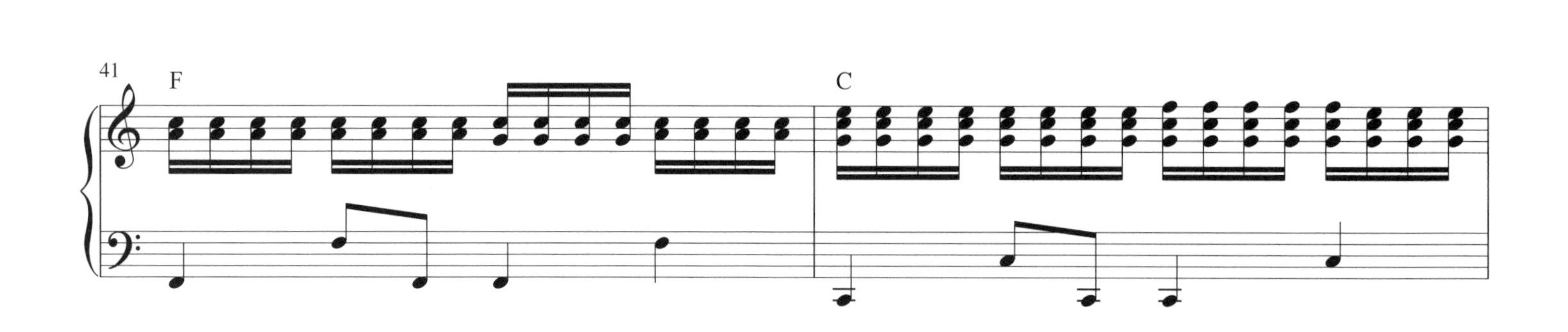
41
F
C

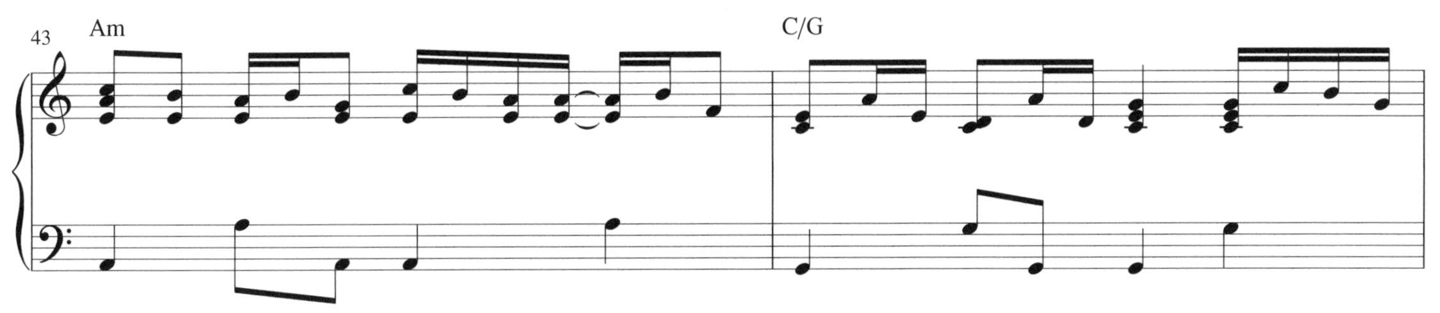
43
Am
C/G

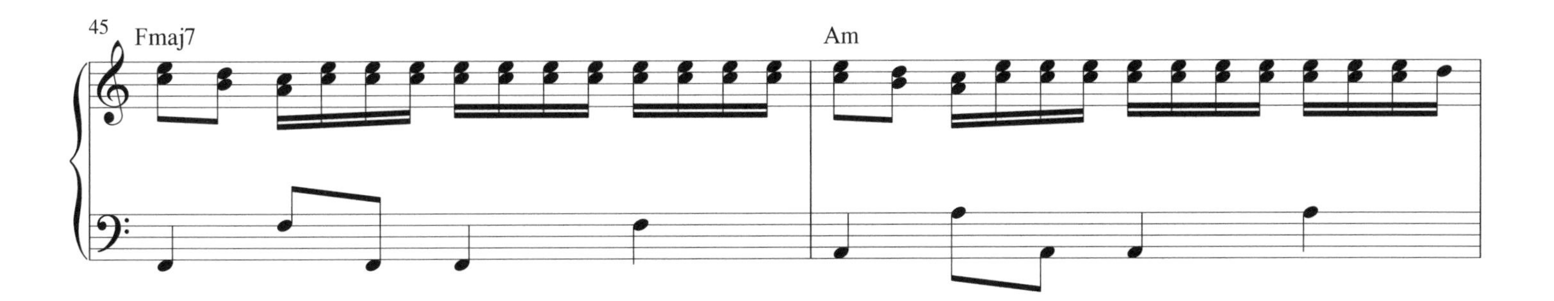
45
Fmaj7
Am

47
G(add2)
Dm7

49
Fsus2
C
Am7
In my heart and my soul, well, I give You con - trol. Con - sume me from the
mp

52
Gsus
Fsus2
Am7
in - side out, Lord. Let jus - tice and praise be - come my em - brace,
cresc. poco a poco

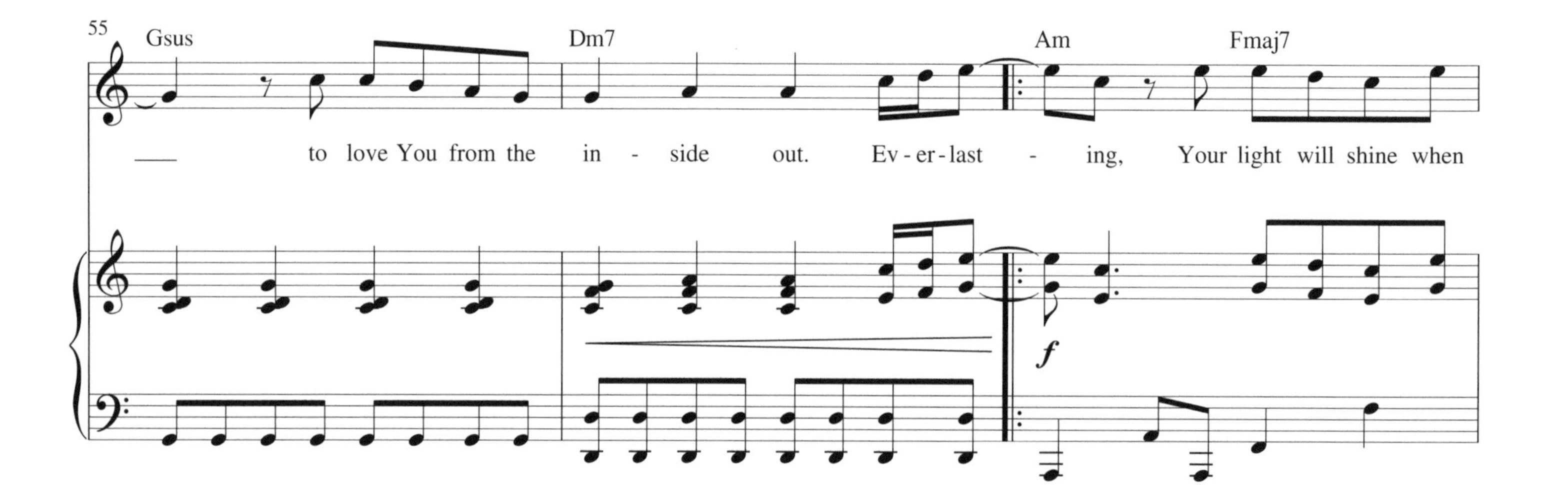
55
Gsus
Dm7
Am
Fmaj7
to love You from the in - side out. Ev - er - last - ing, Your light will shine when
f

58
C
G
Am
Fmaj7
C
G
all else fades. Nev - er - end - ing, Your glo - ry goes be - yond all fame. And the cry

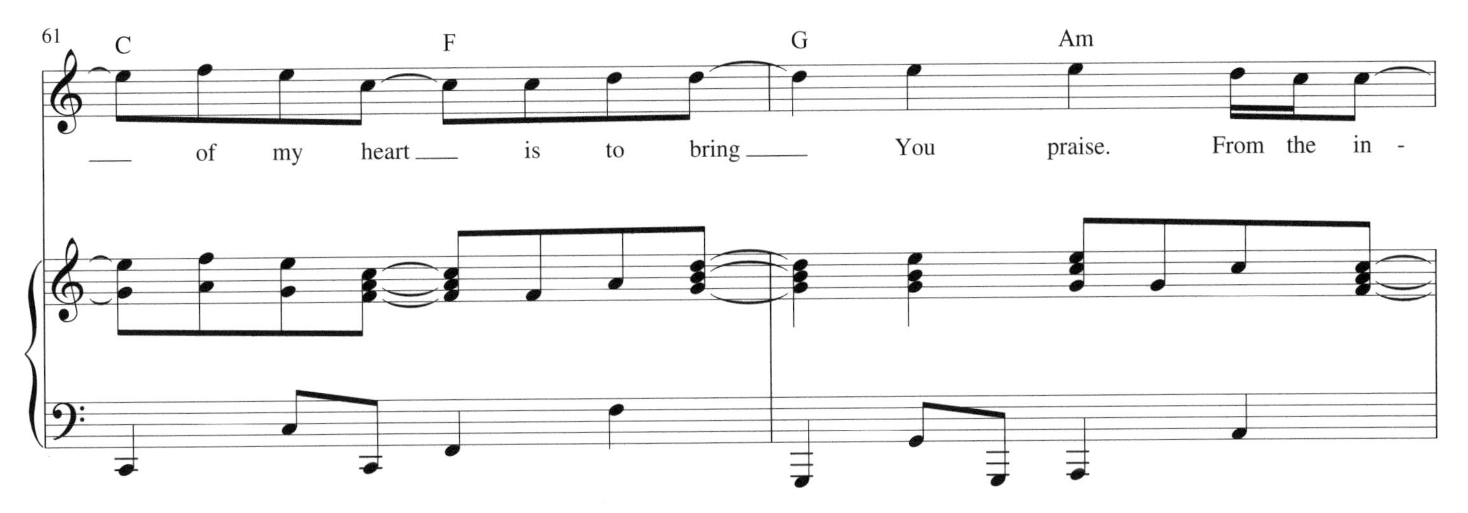
61
C
F
G
Am
of my heart is to bring You praise. From the in -

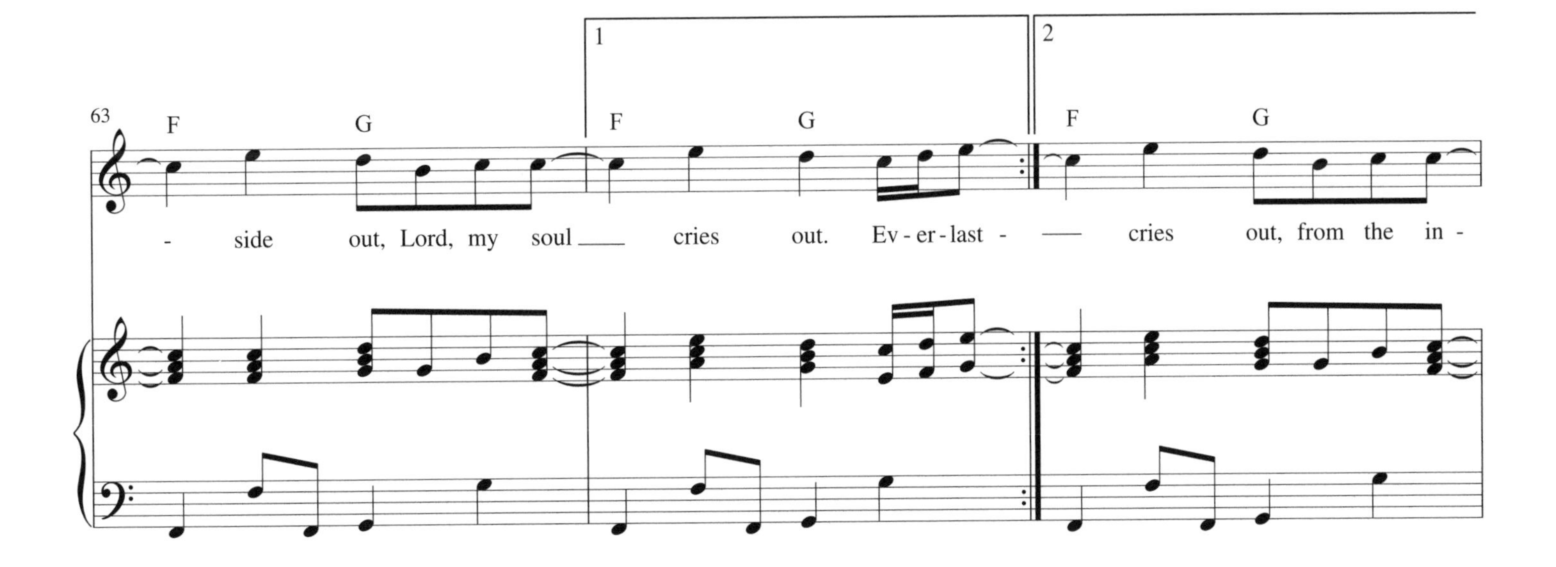
63
1
2
F
G
F
G
F
G
- side out, Lord, my soul cries out. Ev - er - last - cries out, from the in -

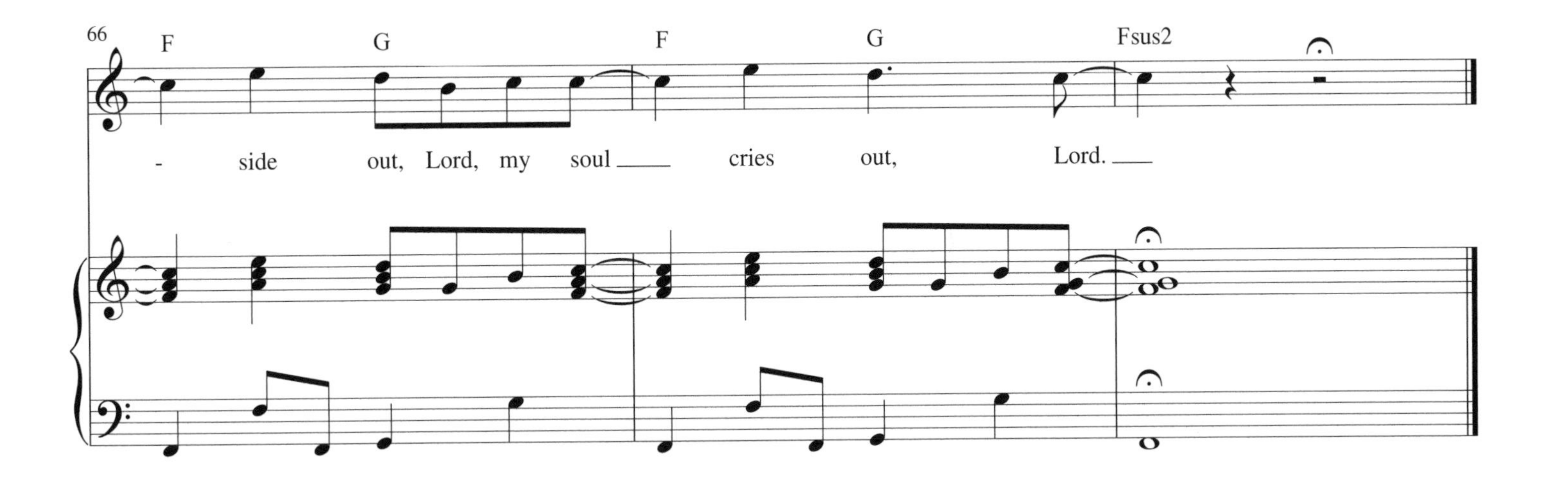
66
F
G
F
G
Fsus2
- side out, Lord, my soul cries out, Lord.

I Will Rise

Words and Music by CHRIS TOMLIN,
JESSE REEVES, LOUIE GIGLIO
and MATT MAHER

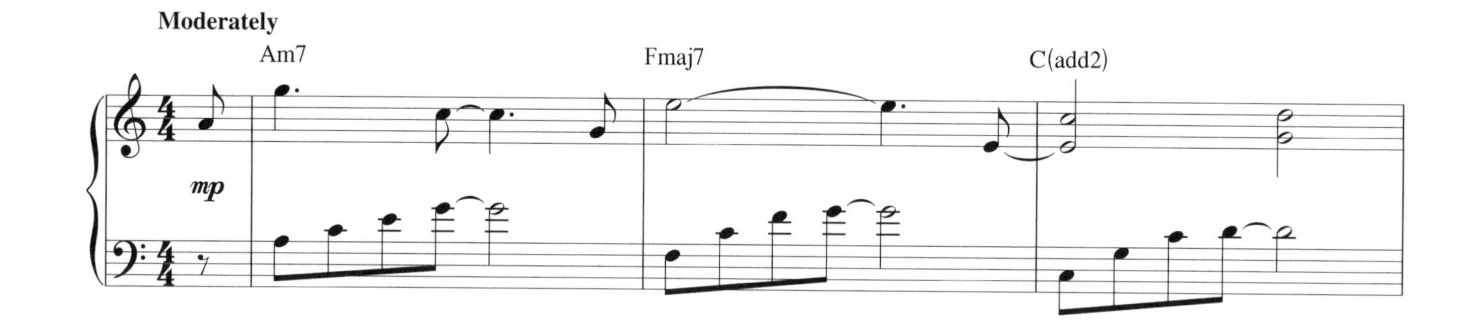

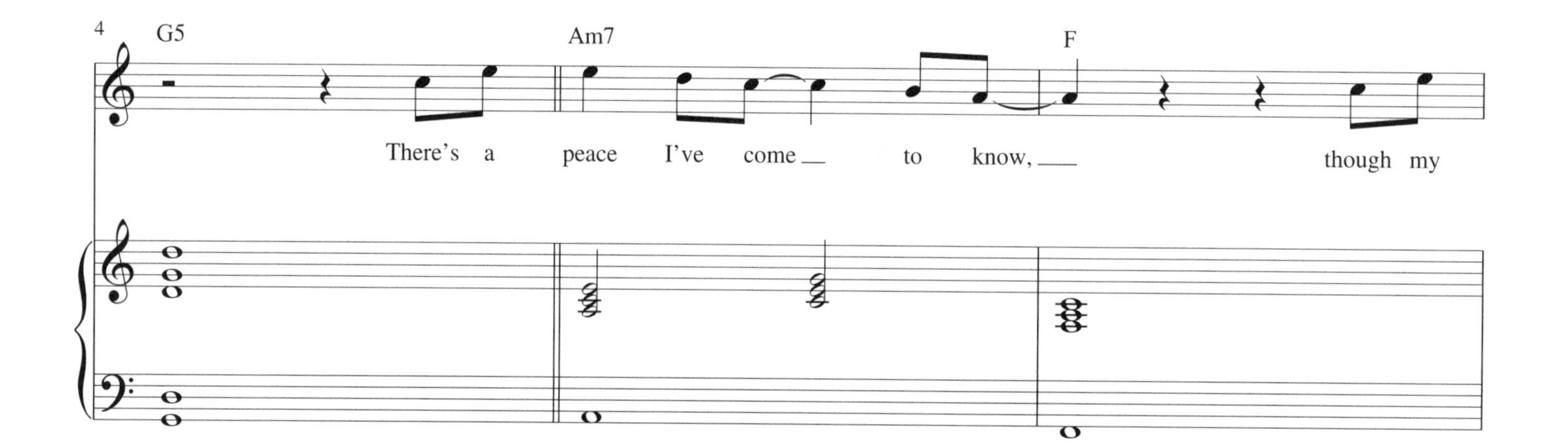

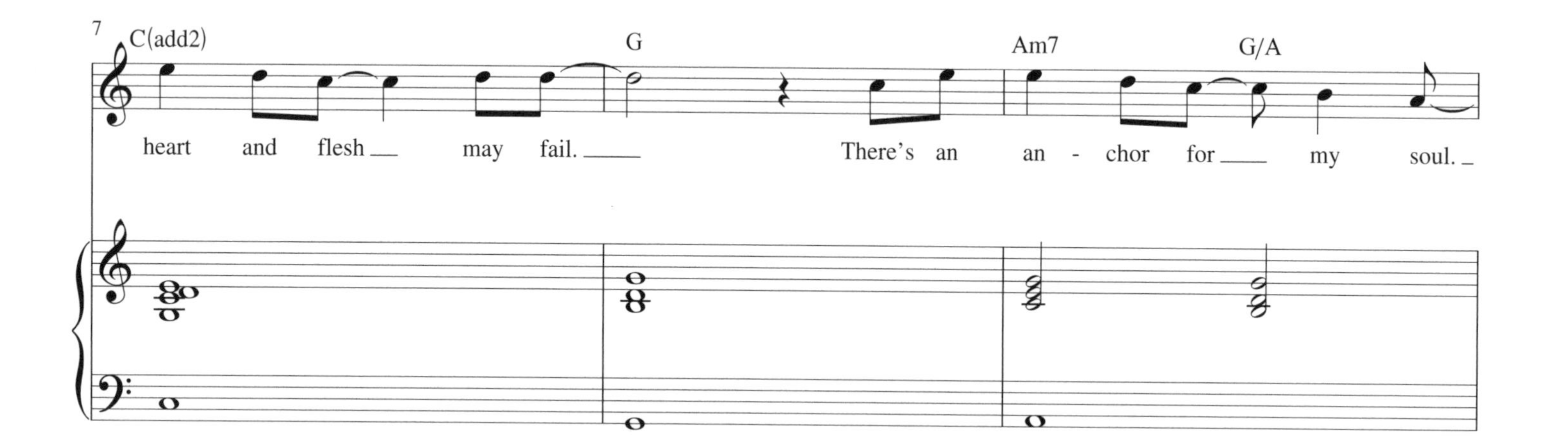

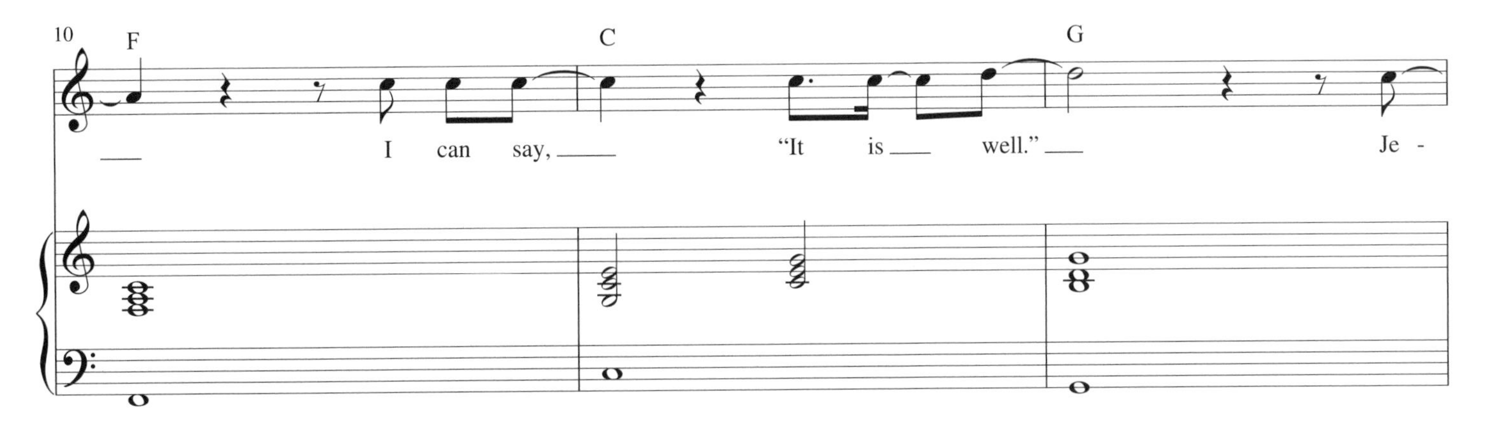
10
F
C
G
I can say, "It is well." Je -

13
C
G/C
Am7
- sus has o - ver - come, and the grave is o - ver - whelmed.

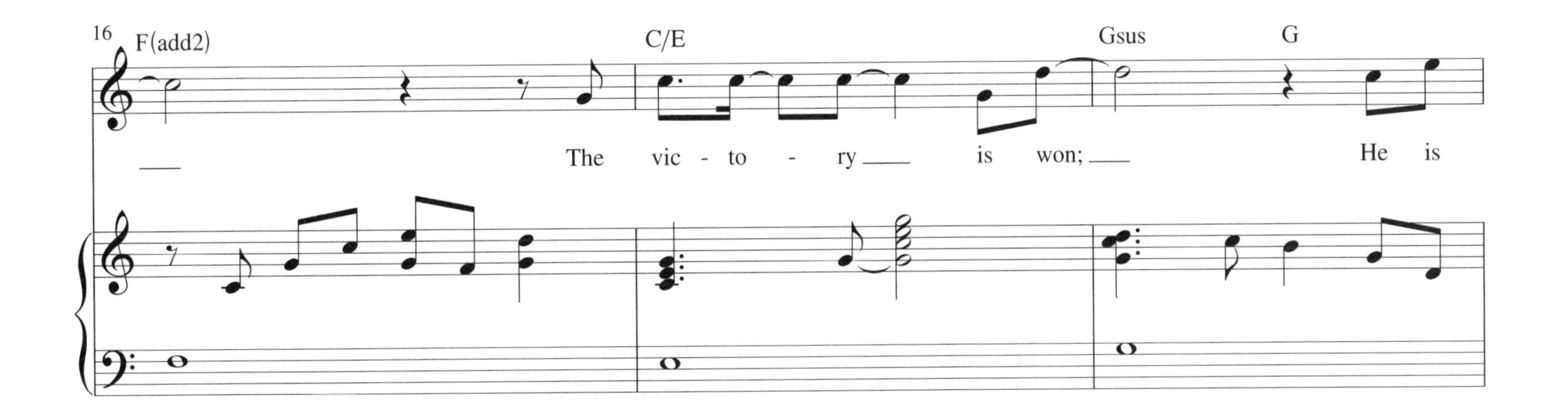
16
F(add2)
C/E
Gsus
G
The vic - to - ry is won; He is

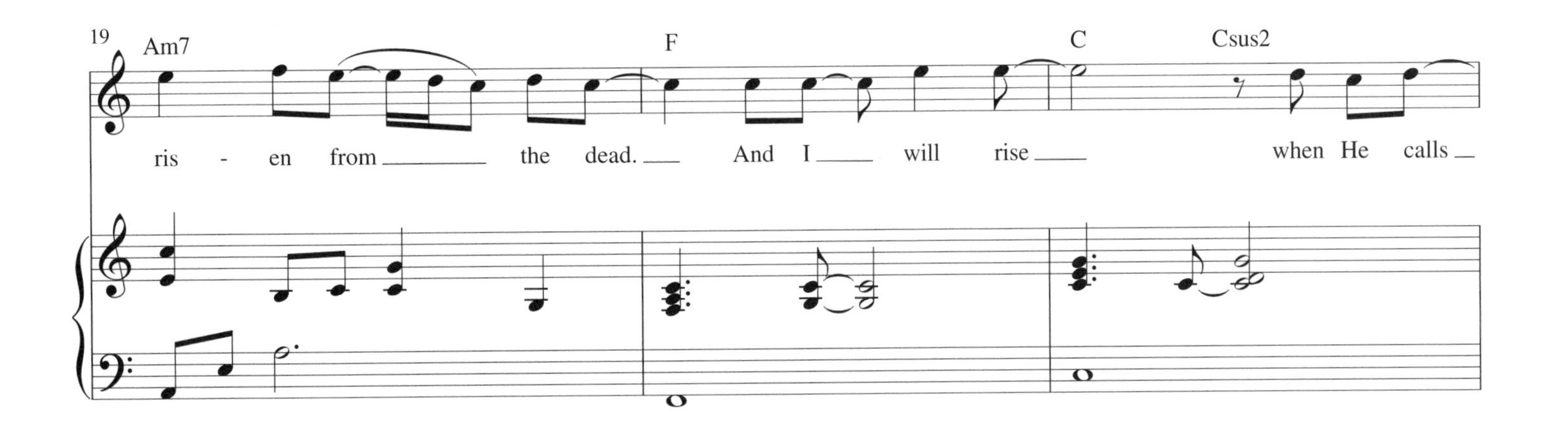
19
Am7
F
C
Csus2
ris - en from the dead. And I will rise when He calls

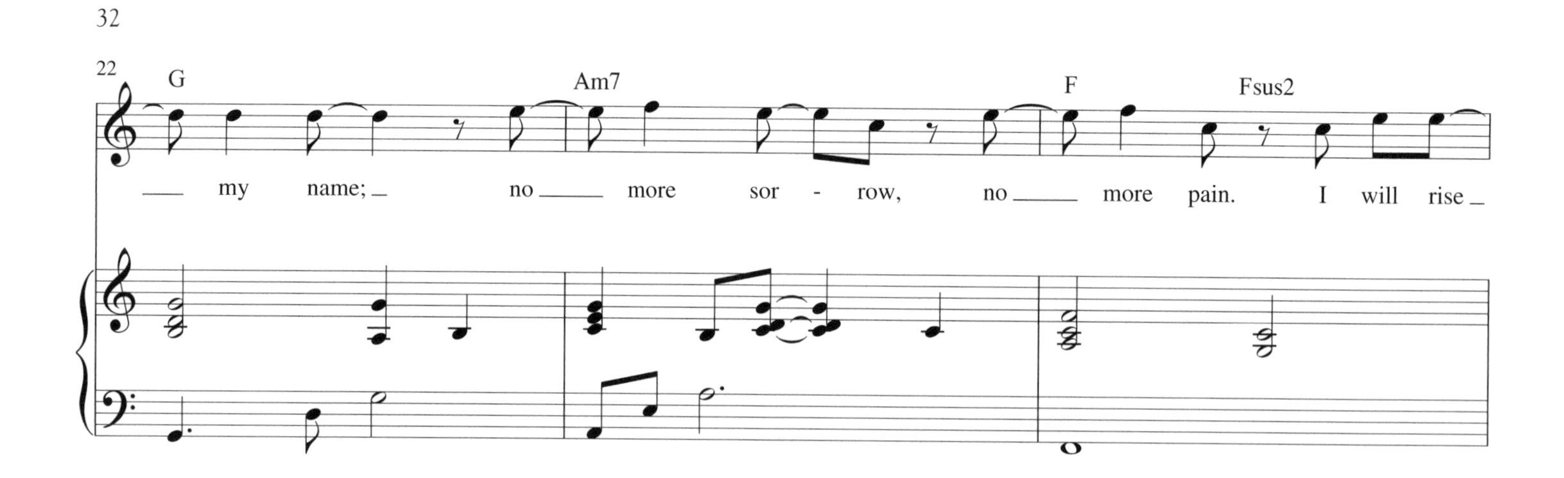
22
G
Am7
F
Fsus2
my name; no more sor - row, no more pain. I will rise

25
C(add2)
G
Am7
on ea - gles' wings, be - fore my God fall on

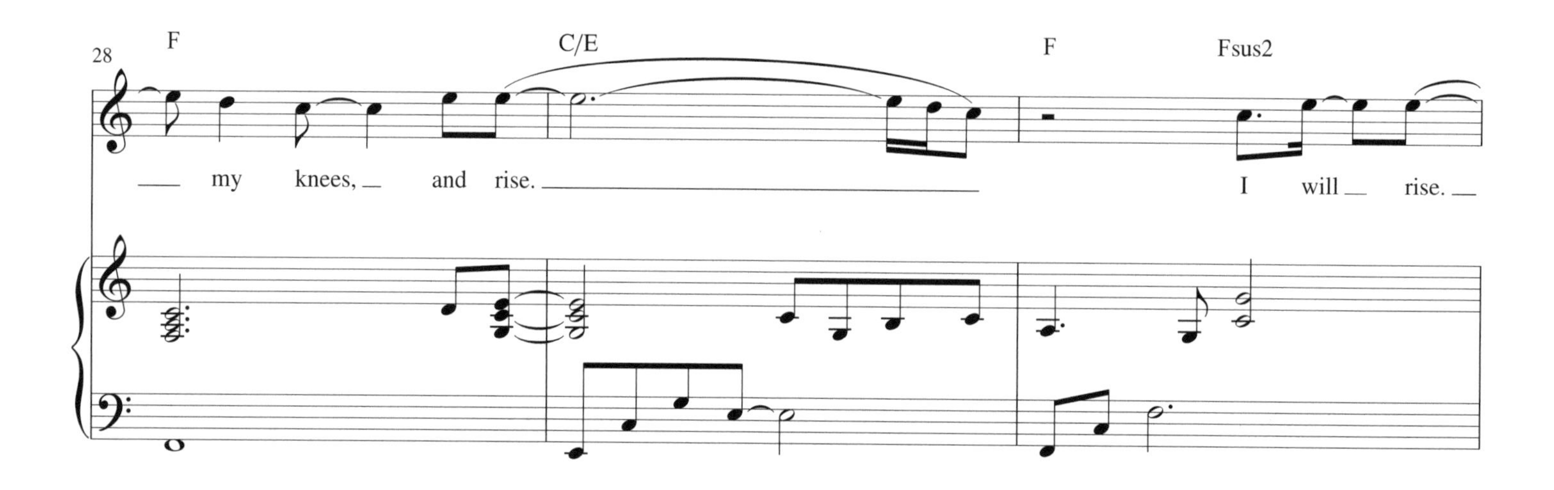
28
F
C/E
F
Fsus2
my knees, and rise. I will rise.

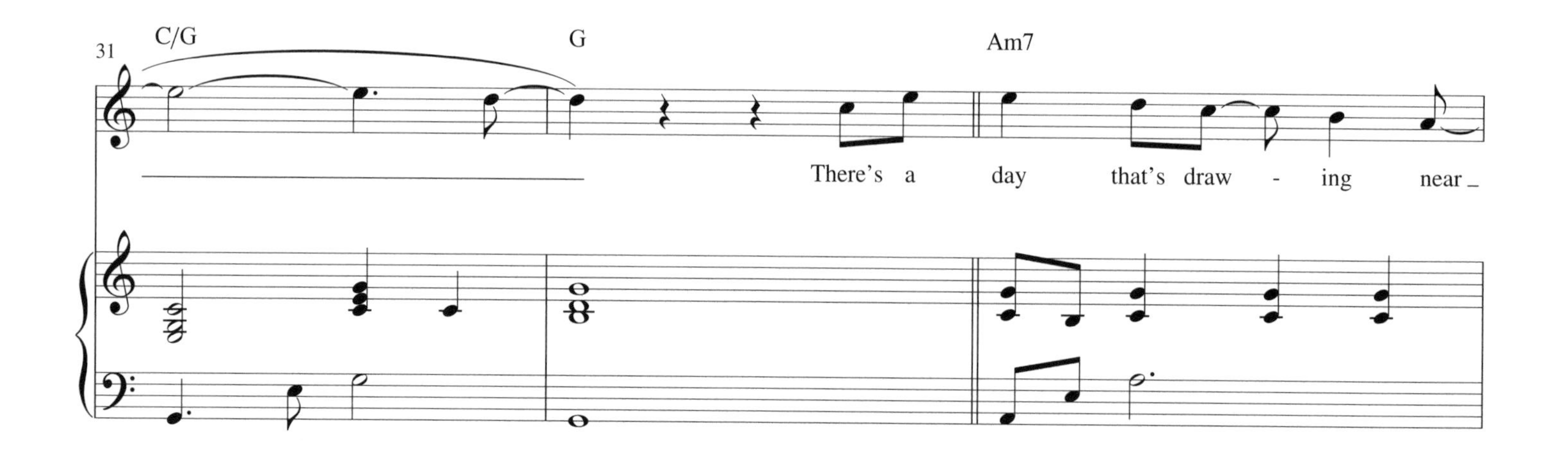
31
C/G
G
Am7
There's a day that's draw - ing near

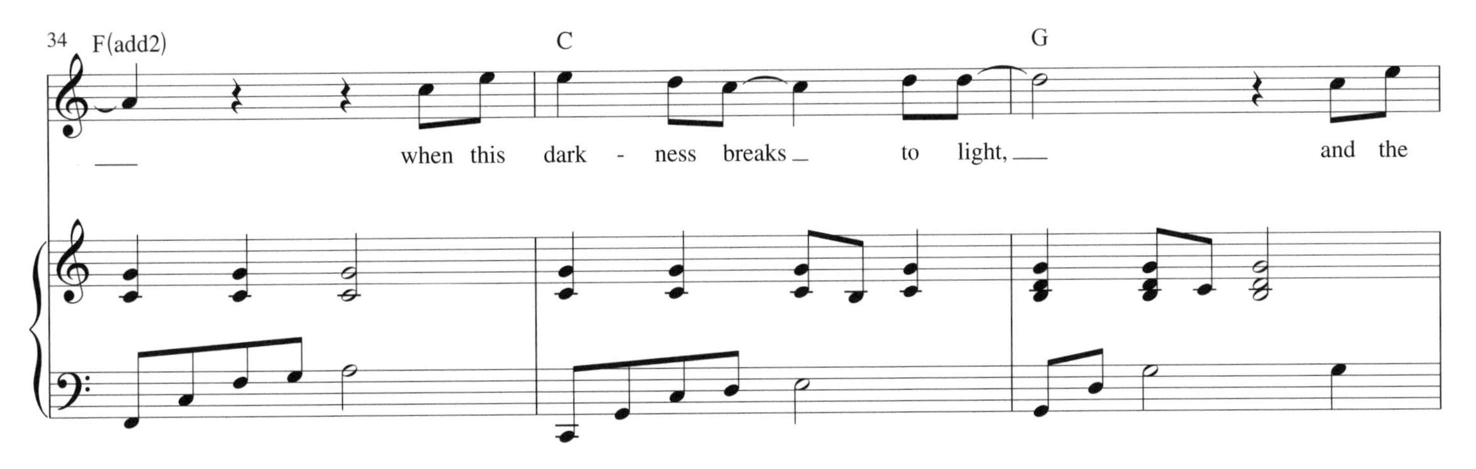
34
F(add2)
C
G
when this dark - ness breaks to light, and the

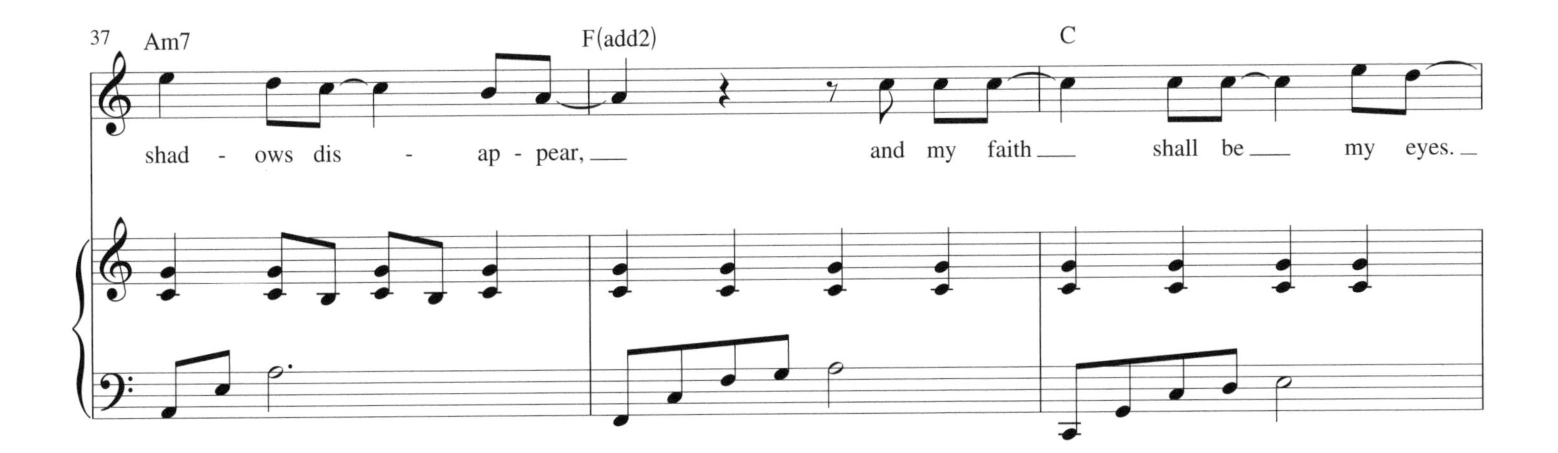
37
Am7
F(add2)
C
shad - ows dis - ap - pear, and my faith shall be my eyes.

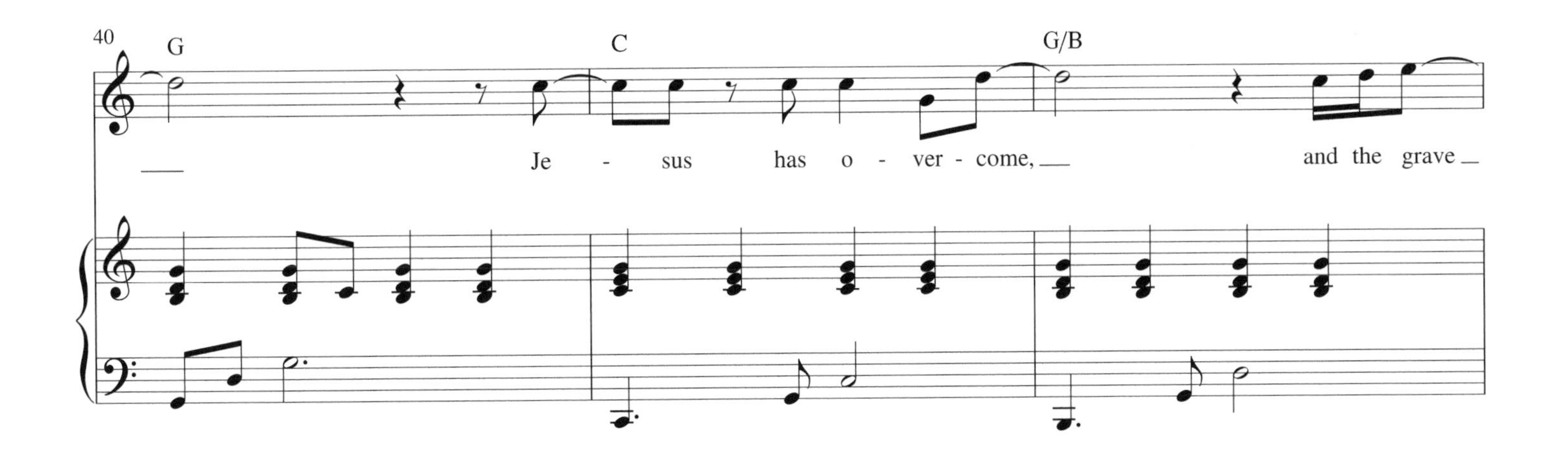
40
G
C
G/B
Je - sus has o - ver - come, and the grave

43
Am7
F
C/E
is o - ver - whelmed. The vic - to - ry is won;

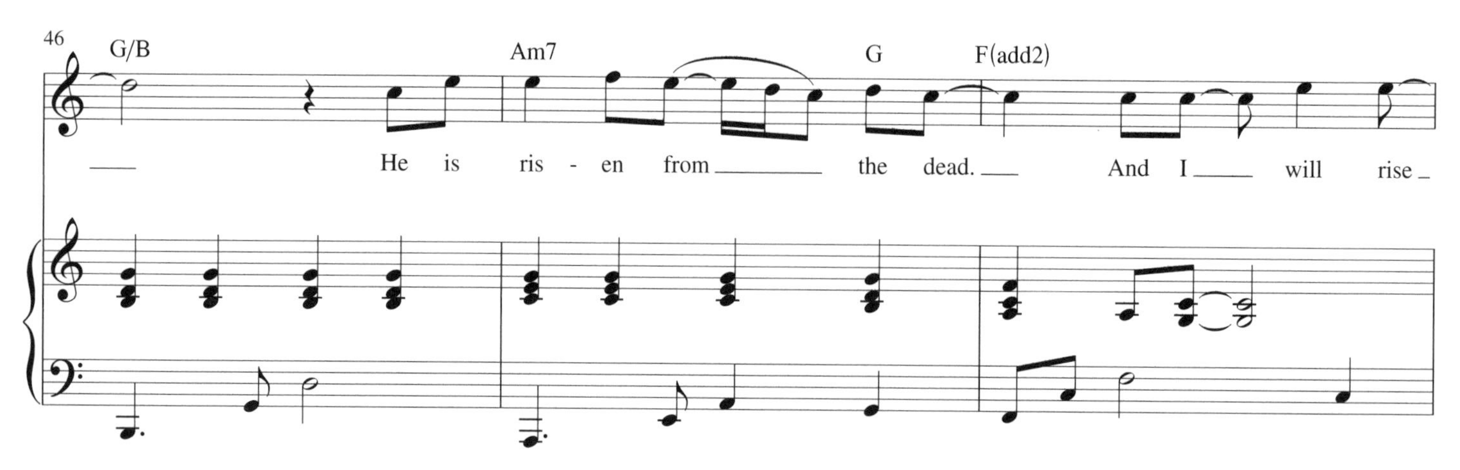
46
G/B
Am7
G
F(add2)
He is ris - en from the dead. And I will rise

49
C
G
Am7
when He calls my name; no more sor - row, no
mf

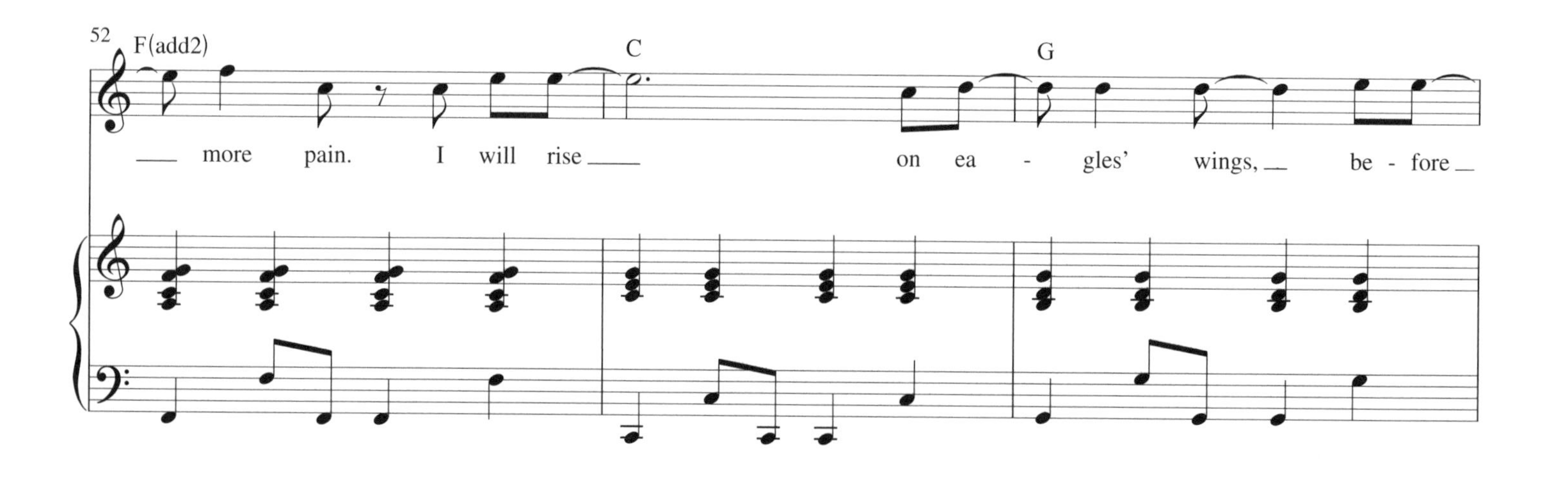
52
F(add2)
C
G
more pain. I will rise on ea - gles' wings, be - fore

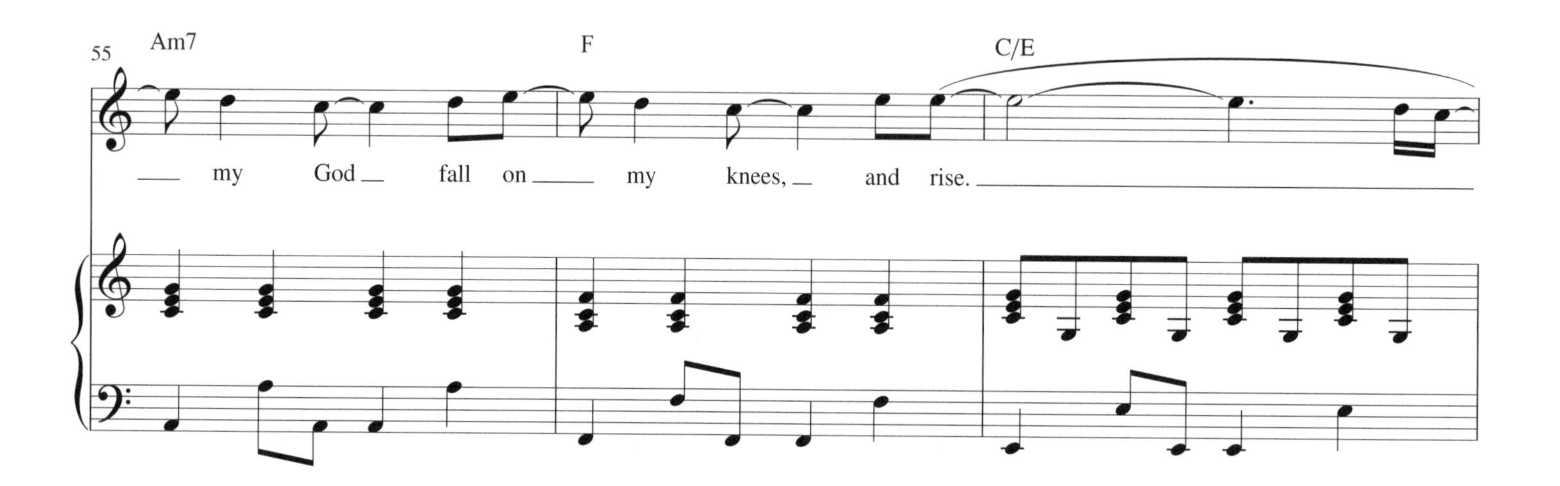
55
Am7
F
C/E
my God fall on my knees, and rise.

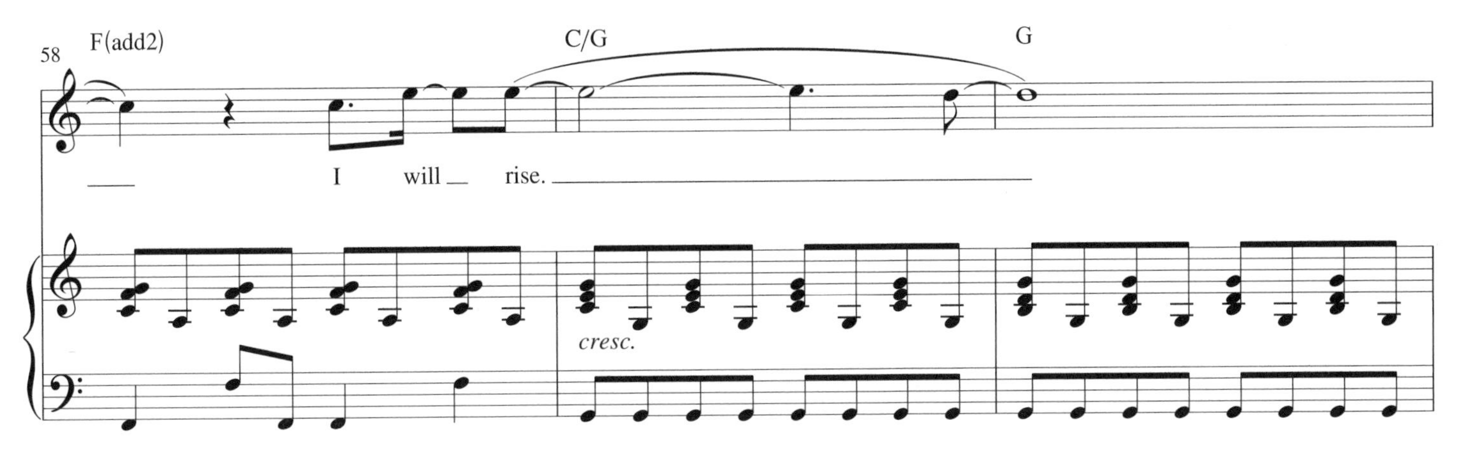
58
F(add2)
C/G
G
I will rise.
cresc.

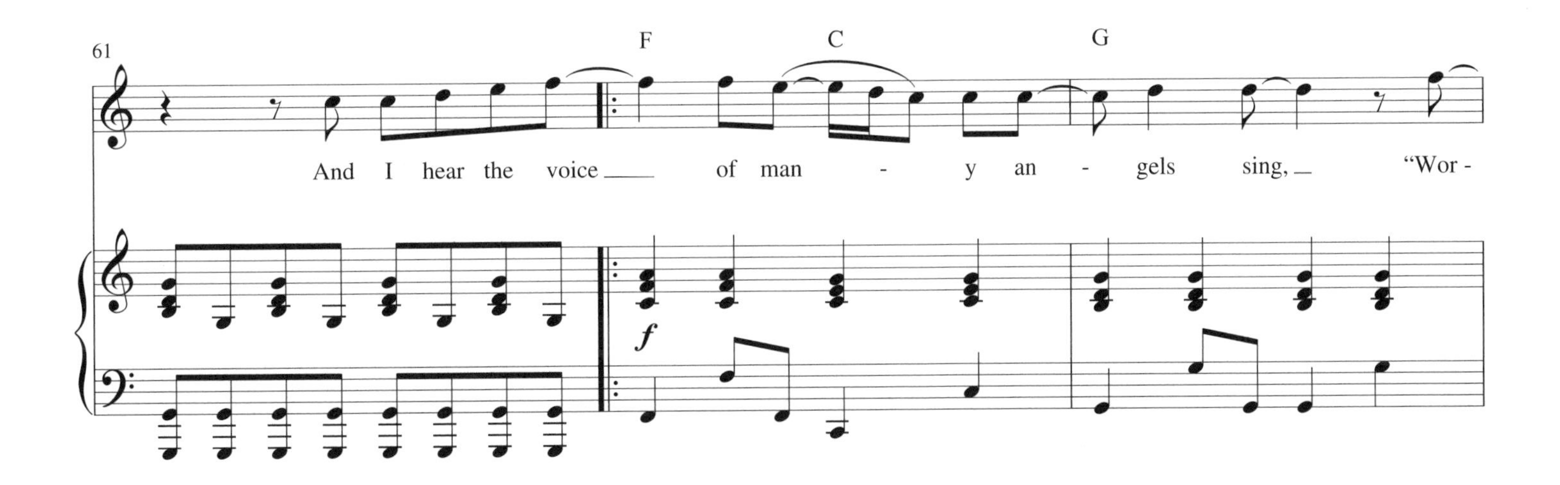
61
F
C
G
And I hear the voice of man - y an - gels sing, "Wor -
f

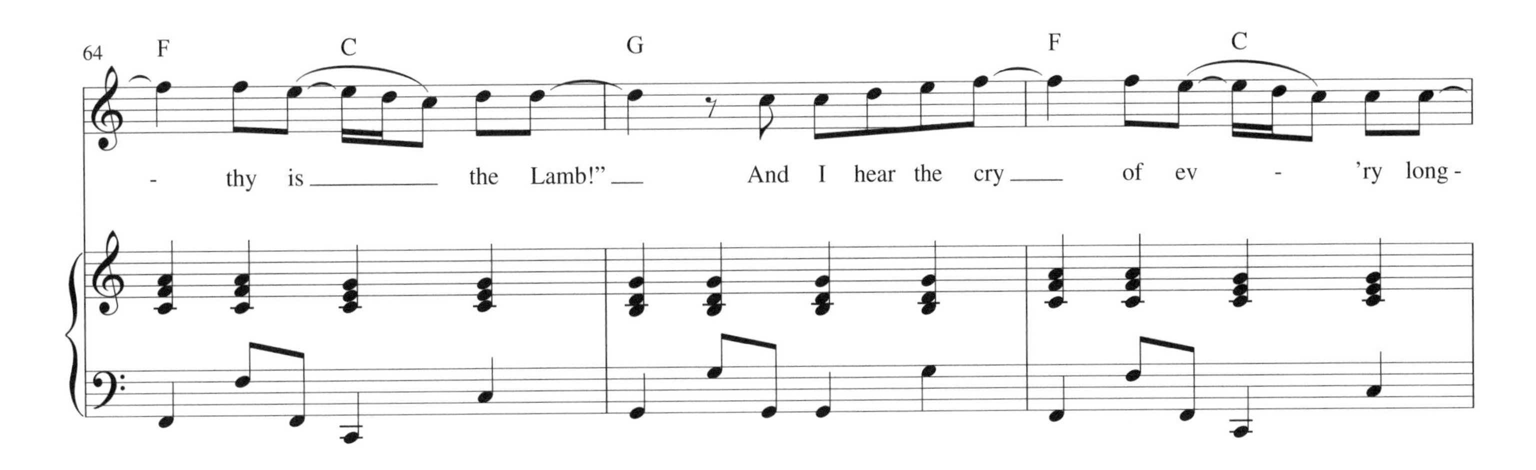
64
F
C
G
F
C
- thy is the Lamb!" And I hear the cry of ev - 'ry long -

1
67
G
F
C
G
- ing heart, "Wor - thy is the Lamb!" And I hear the voice

2
70
G
Am7
F
C
-ing heart, "Wor-thy is the Lamb!

72
G
F
C
G
Wor-thy is the Lamb!"

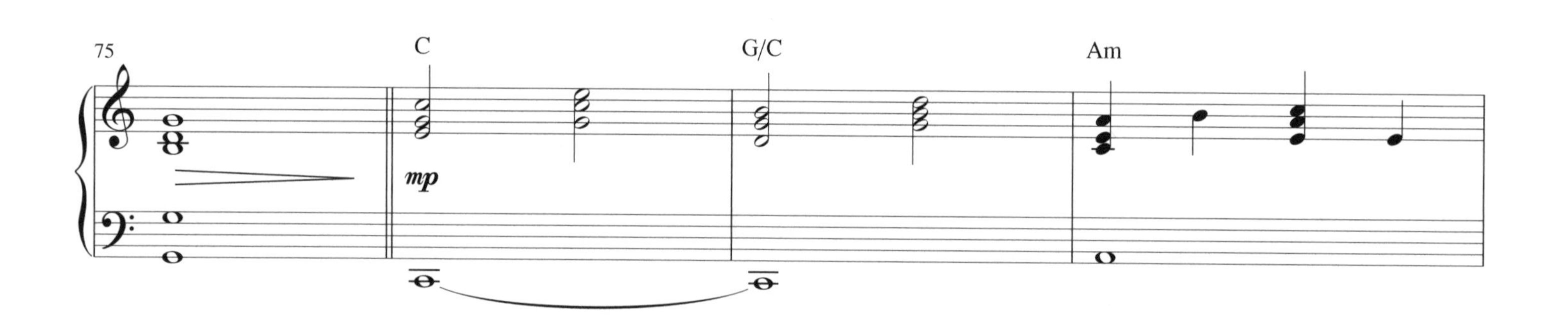
75
C
G/C
Am
mp

79
F
C
G
I will rise when He calls my name; no

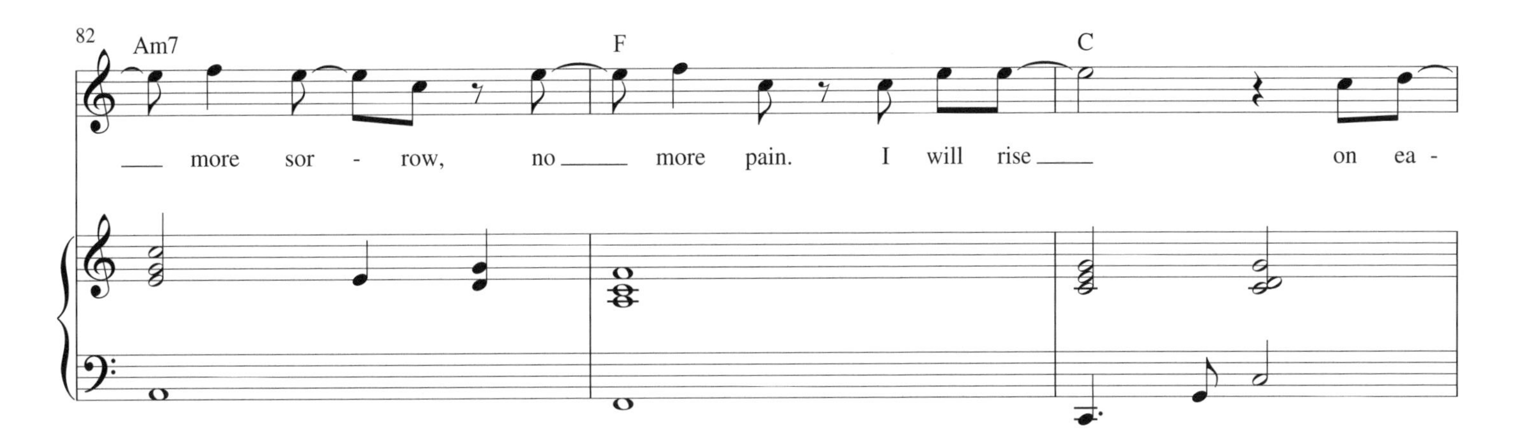
82
Am7
F
C
more sor - row, no more pain. I will rise on ea -

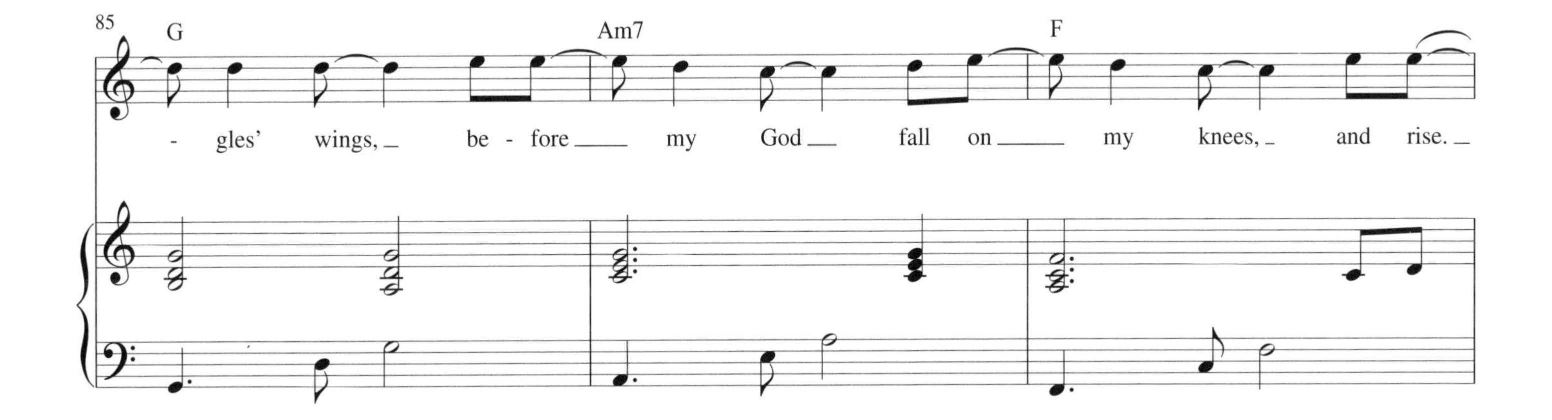
85
G
Am7
F
- gles' wings, be - fore my God fall on my knees, and rise.

88
C/E
F
C/G
I will rise.

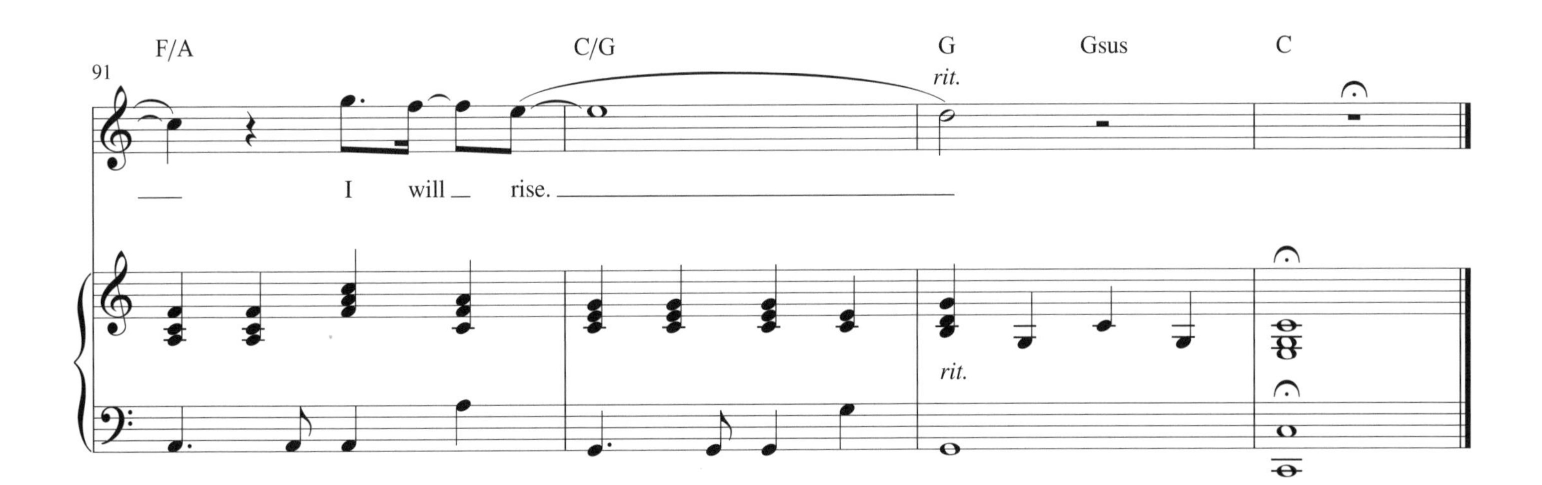
91
F/A
C/G
G
Gsus
C
rit.
I will rise.
rit.

Lead Me to the Cross

Words and Music by
BROOKE FRASER

13
Am
D
Em
Dsus
And ev - 'ry - thing I once held dear, I count it all as loss.

16
Csus2
Cmaj9
G
D
Lead me to the cross where Your love poured out. Bring me to my knees.

19
Cmaj9
G
D
Cmaj9
G
Lord, I lay me down. Rid me of my - self. I be - long to You.

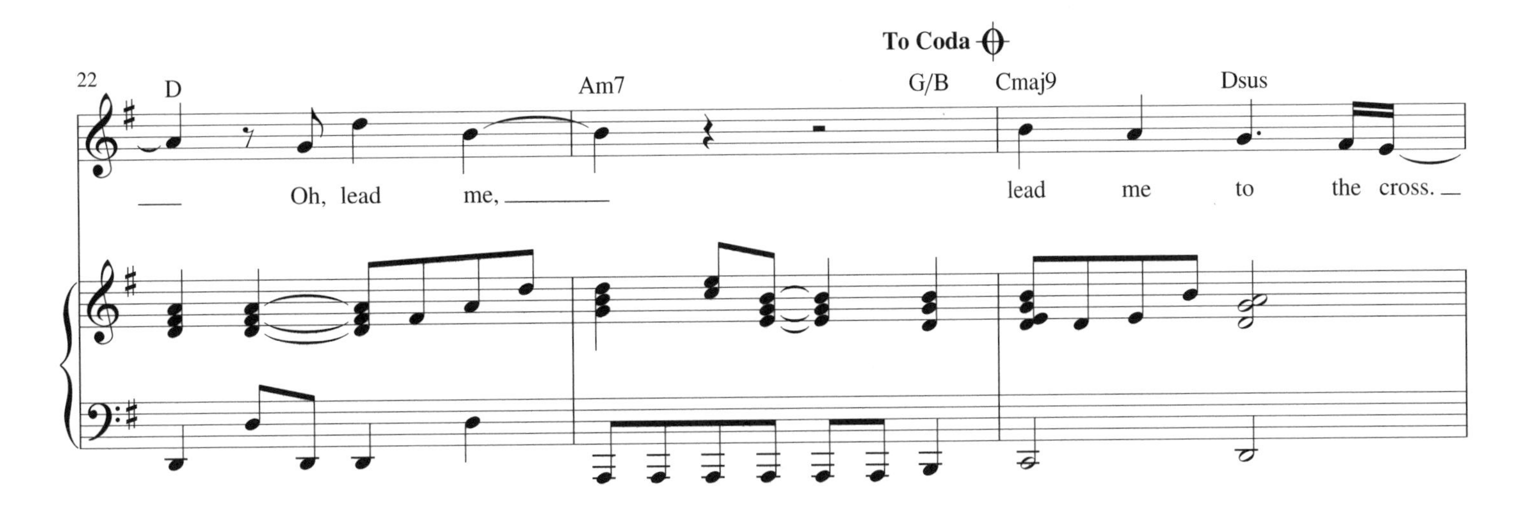
To Coda
22
D
Am7
G/B
Cmaj9
Dsus
Oh, lead me, lead me to the cross.

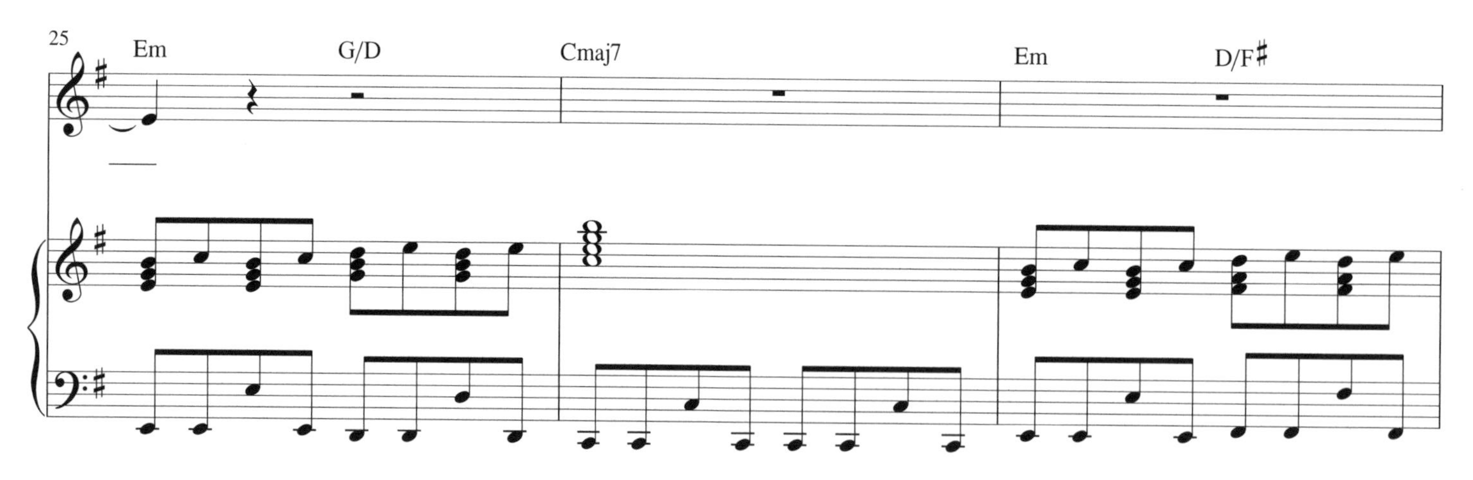
25
Em
G/D
Cmaj7
Em
D/F♯

28
C6
Em7
D
You were, as I,
tempt - ed and tried,

31
Cmaj7
G
D/F♯
Em7
hu - man.
Word be - came flesh,

34
D
Cmaj7
G/B
D
bore my sin and death.
Now You're ris - en.

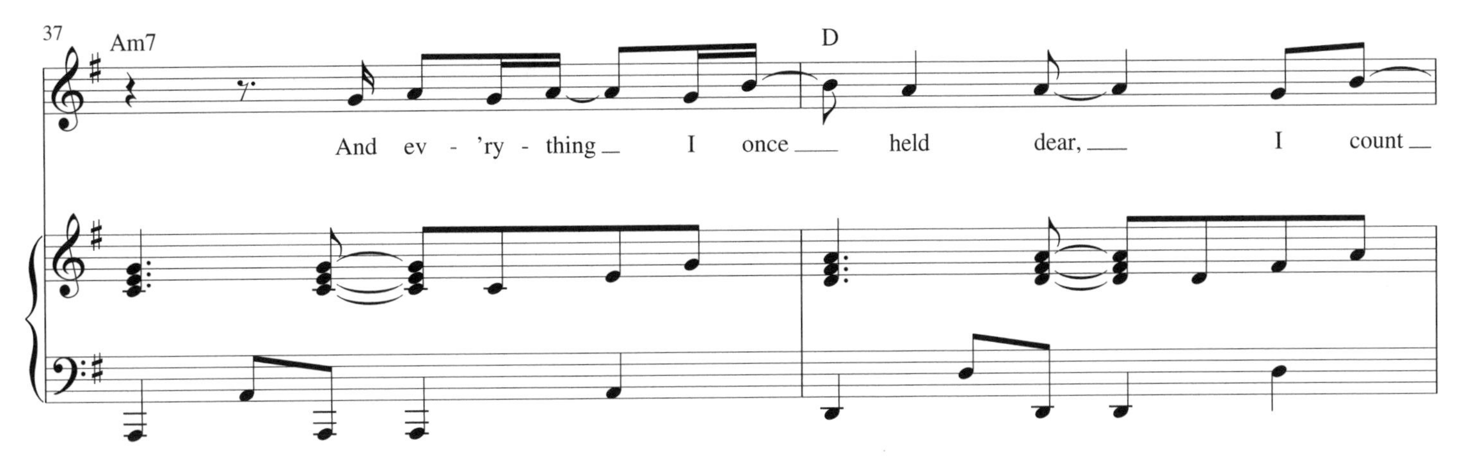
37
Am7
D
And ev - 'ry - thing I once held dear, I count

39
Em
D
Cmaj7
N.C.
D.S. al Coda
it all as loss. Lead me to the cross

CODA
Cmaj9
Dsus
G
Cmaj7
41
lead me to Your heart.

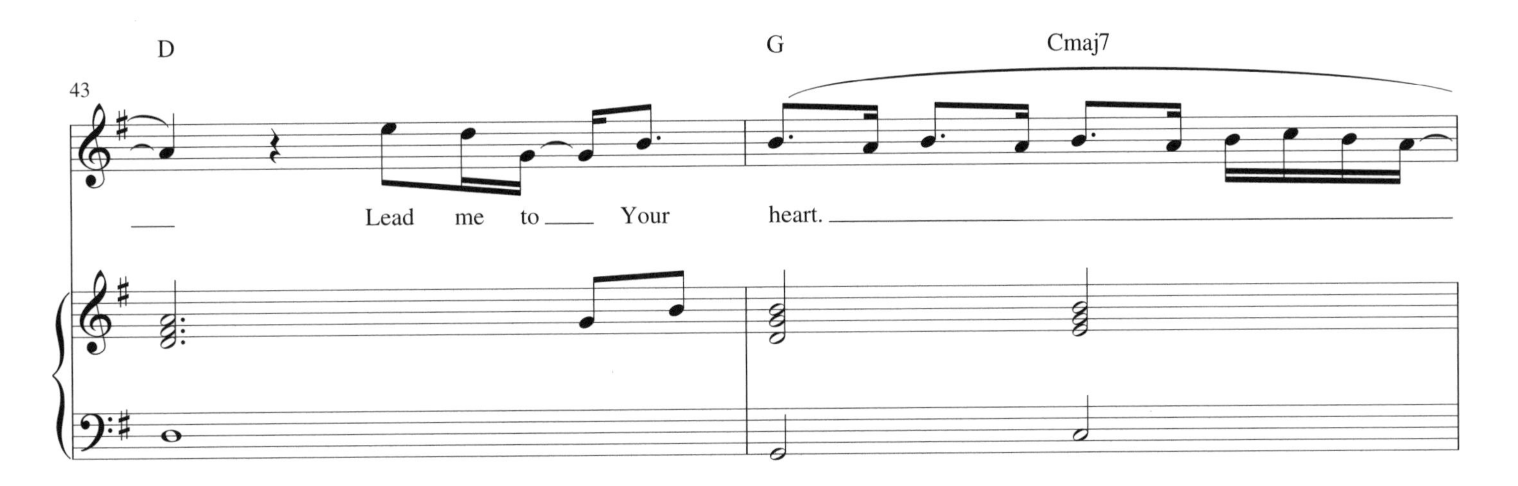
D
G
Cmaj7
43
Lead me to Your heart.

D
Em
Cmaj7
45
Lead me to Your heart.

D
Em7
Cmaj9
47
Lead me to Your heart.

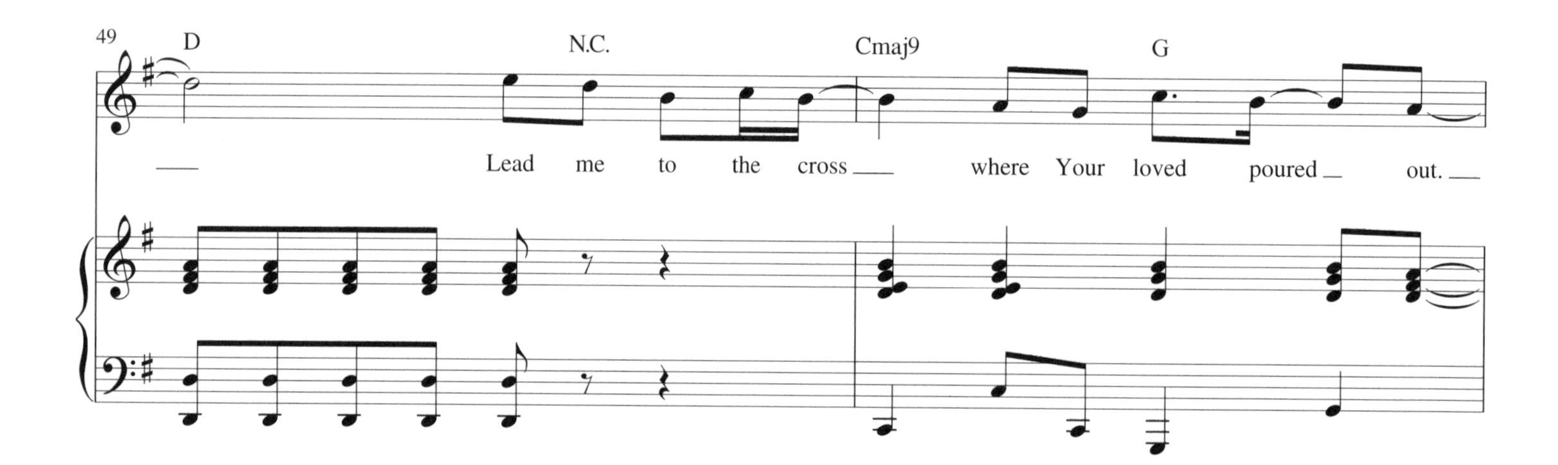

49
D
N.C.
Cmaj9
G
Lead me to the cross where Your loved poured out.

51
D
Cmaj9
G
Bring me to my knees. Lord, I lay me down.

53
D
Cmaj9
G
Rid me of my - self. I be - long to You.

55
D
Am7
G/B
C
Oh, lead me, lead me,

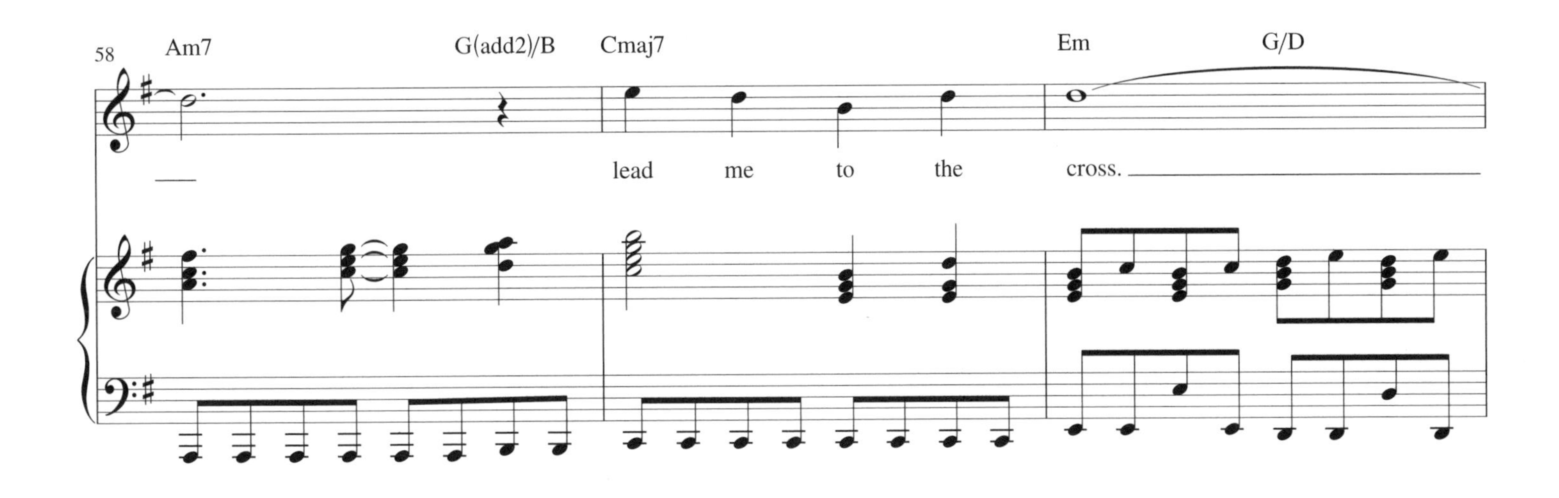
58
Am7
G(add2)/B
Cmaj7
Em
G/D
lead me to the cross.

61
Cmaj7
Em
G/D
C6
Lead me to the cross.

The Potter's Hand

Words and Music by
DARLENE ZSCHECH

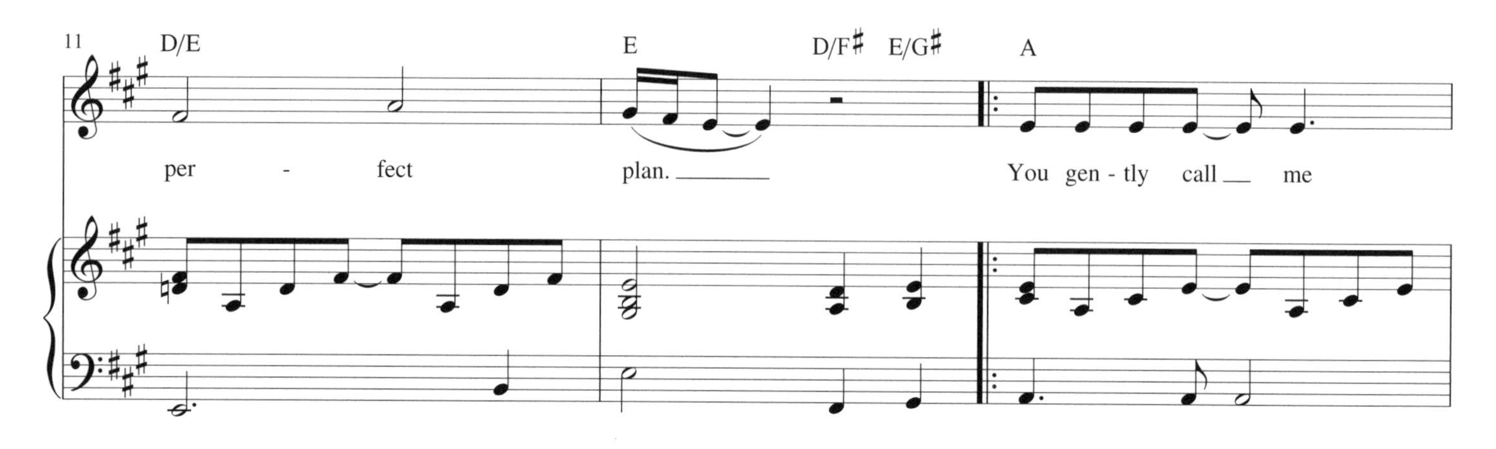

14
E/G♯
D/F♯
Dm/F
in - to Your pres - ence, guid - ing me by Your Ho - ly Spir - it.

17
F♯m
A/B
B/D♯
D/E
Teach me, dear Lord, to live all of my life through Your

20
E
F♯m
E/G♯
eyes. I'm cap - tured by Your ho - ly call - ing.

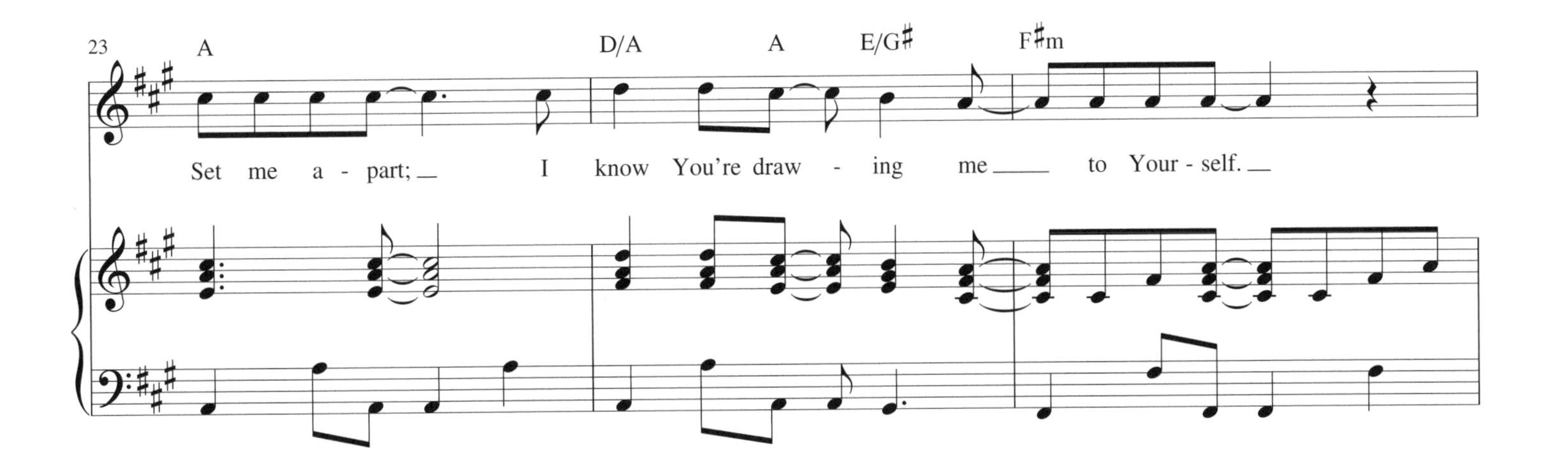
23
A
D/A
A
E/G♯
F♯m
Set me a - part; I know You're draw - ing me to Your - self.

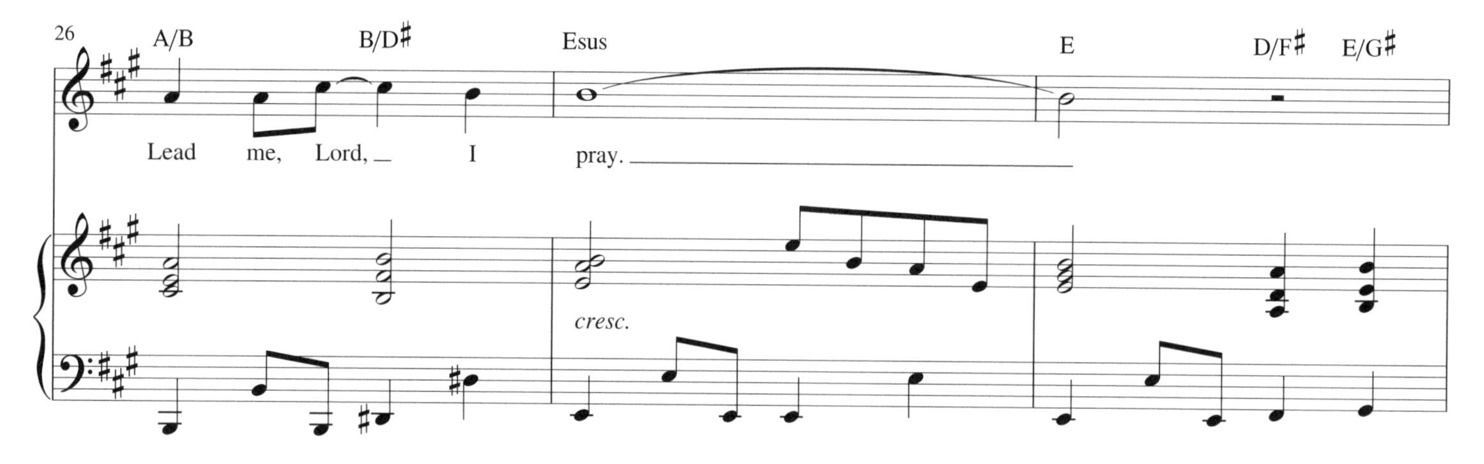
26
A/B
B/D♯
Esus
E
D/F♯
E/G♯
Lead me, Lord, I pray.
cresc.

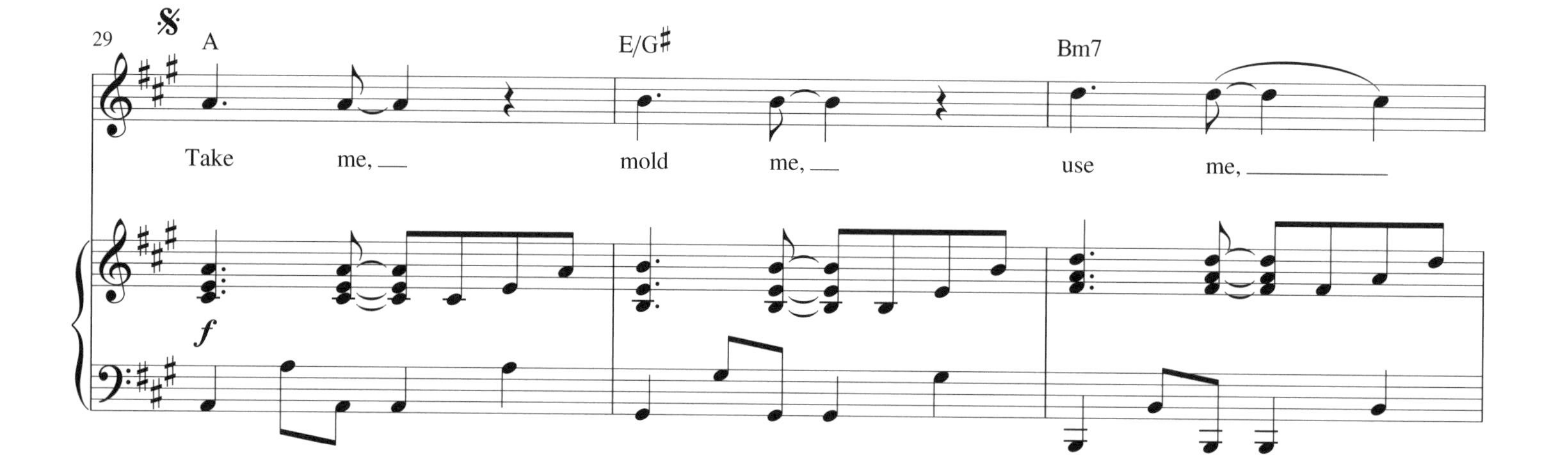
29
A
E/G♯
Bm7
Take me, mold me, use me,
f

32
C♯m/F♯
F♯m7
G
D/F♯
fill me. I give my life to the Pot - ter's hand.

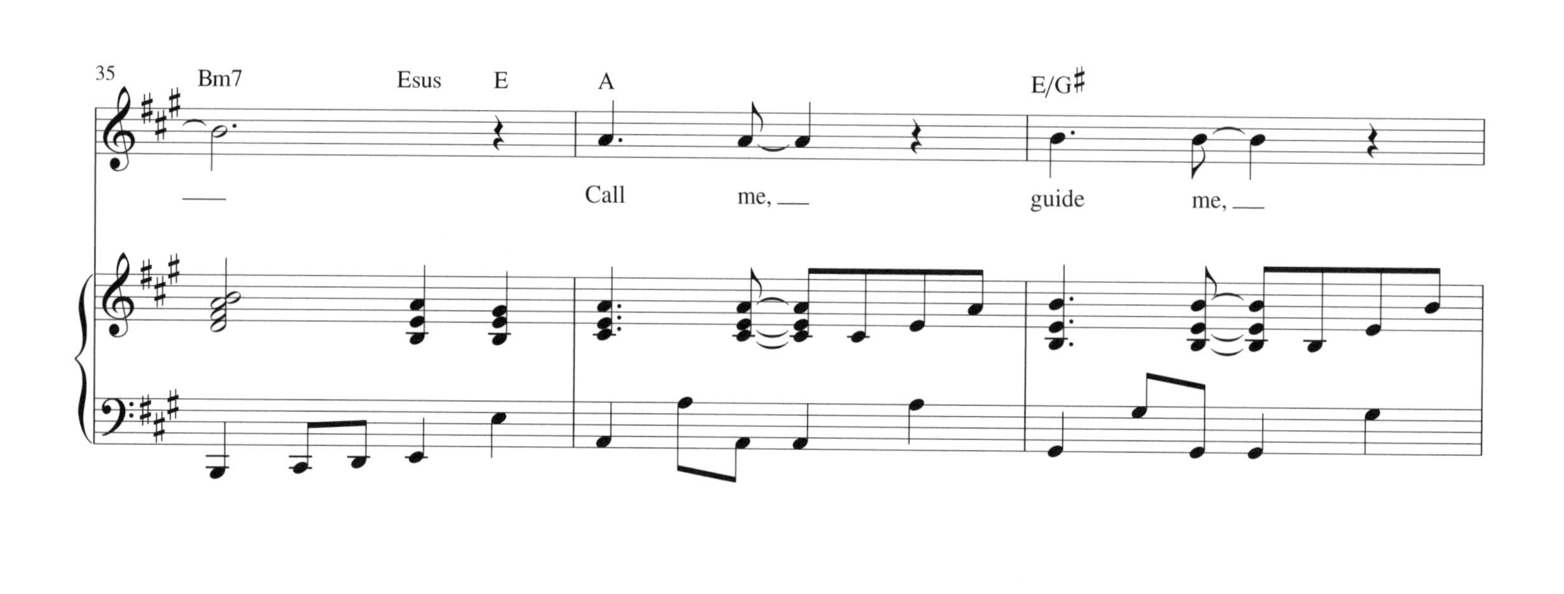
35
Bm7
Esus
E
A
E/G♯
Call me, guide me,

38
Bm7
C♯m/F♯
F♯m7
G
lead me, walk be - side me. I give my life

41
D/F♯
To Coda
1
Bm7
Esus
E
2
D.S. al Coda
Bm7
D/E
E
to the Pot - ter's hand.
dim.

CODA
45
Bm7
D/E
A
F♯m7
Ooh, ooh,
dim.
mp

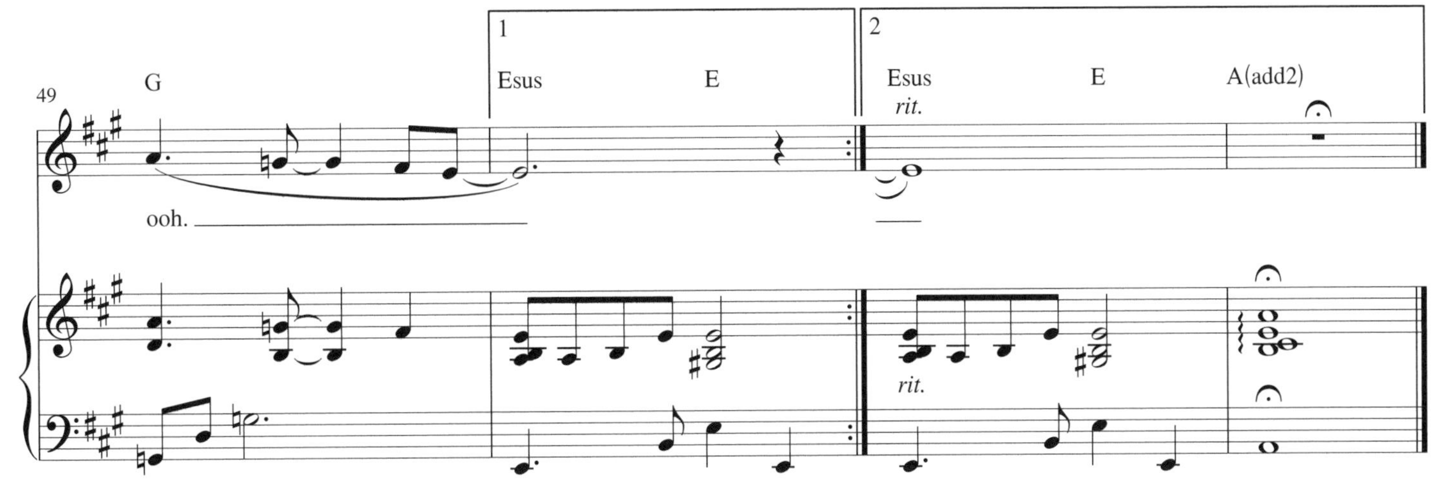
49
G
1
Esus
E
2
Esus
E
A(add2)
rit.
ooh.
rit.

The Power of the Cross
(Oh to See the Dawn)

Words and Music by KEITH GETTY
and STUART TOWNEND

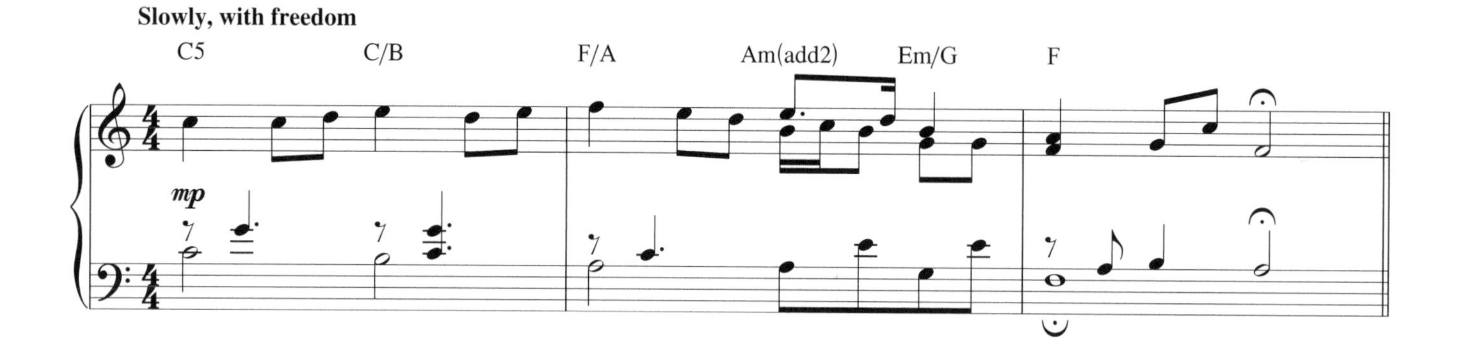

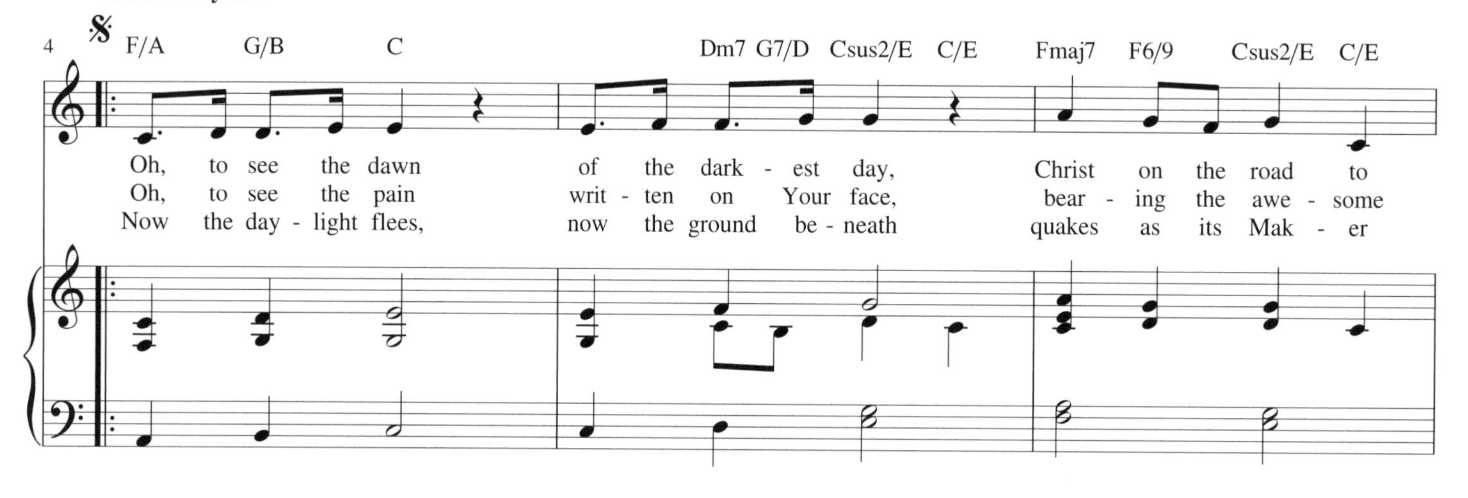

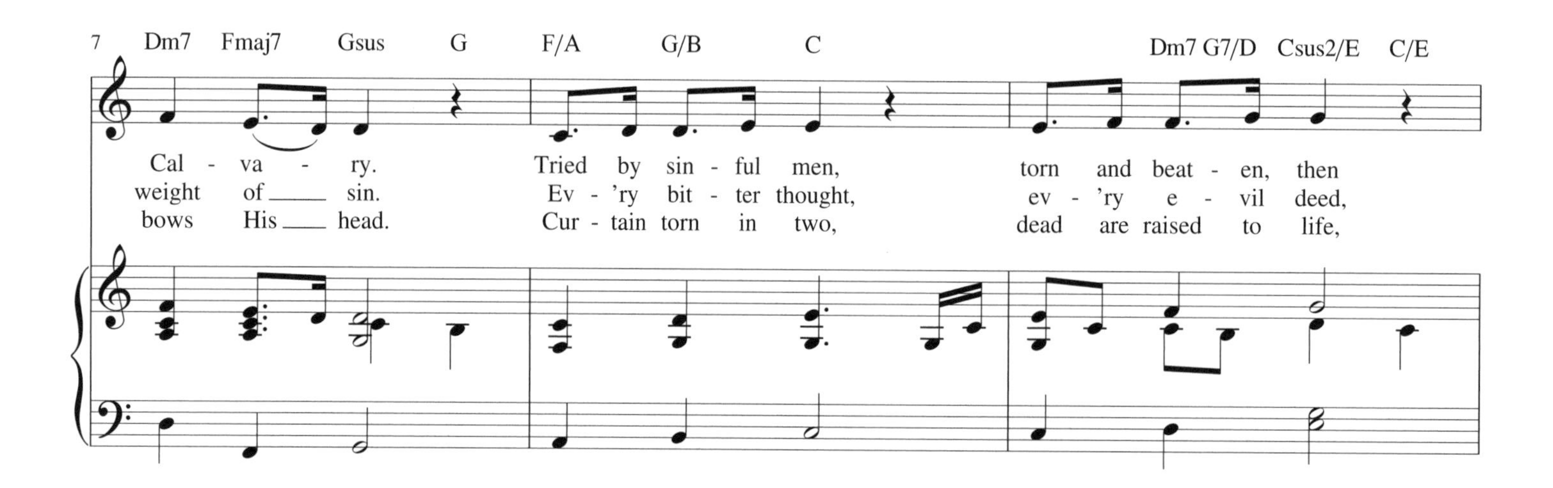

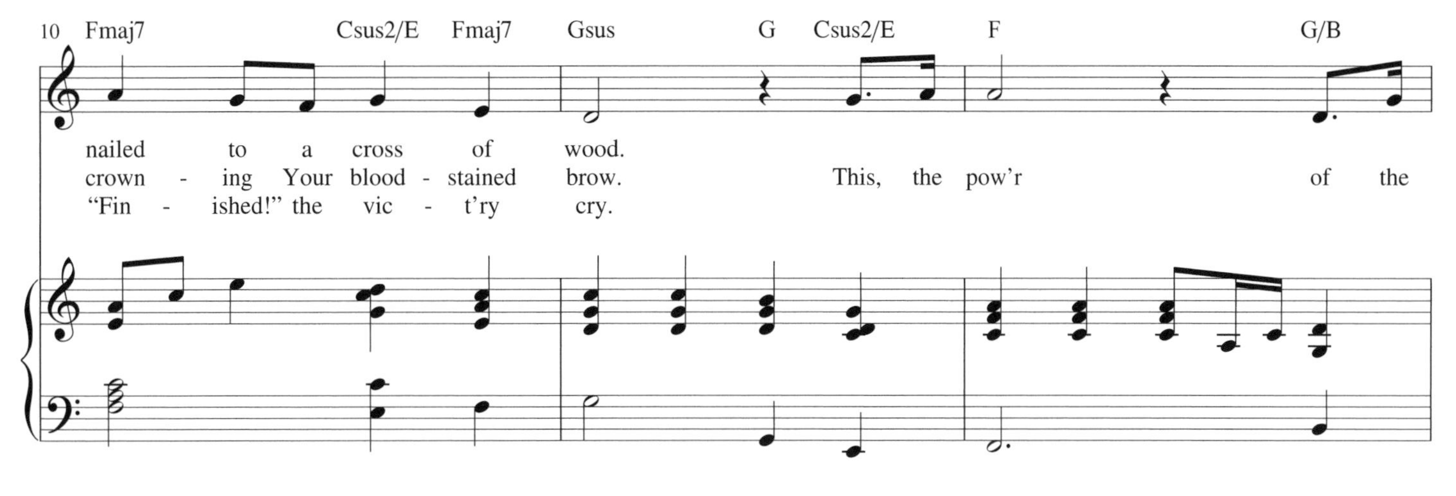
10
Fmaj7 Csus2/E Fmaj7 Gsus G Csus2/E F G/B
nailed to a cross of wood.
crown - ing Your blood - stained brow. This, the pow'r of the
"Fin - ished!" the vic - t'ry cry.

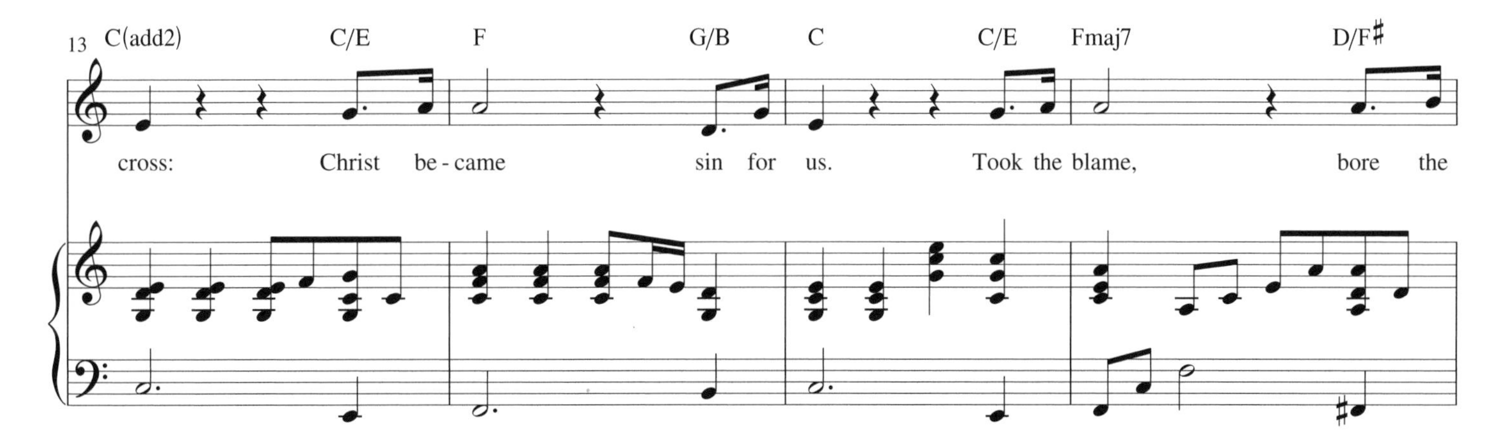
13
C(add2) C/E F G/B C C/E Fmaj7 D/F♯
cross: Christ be-came sin for us. Took the blame, bore the

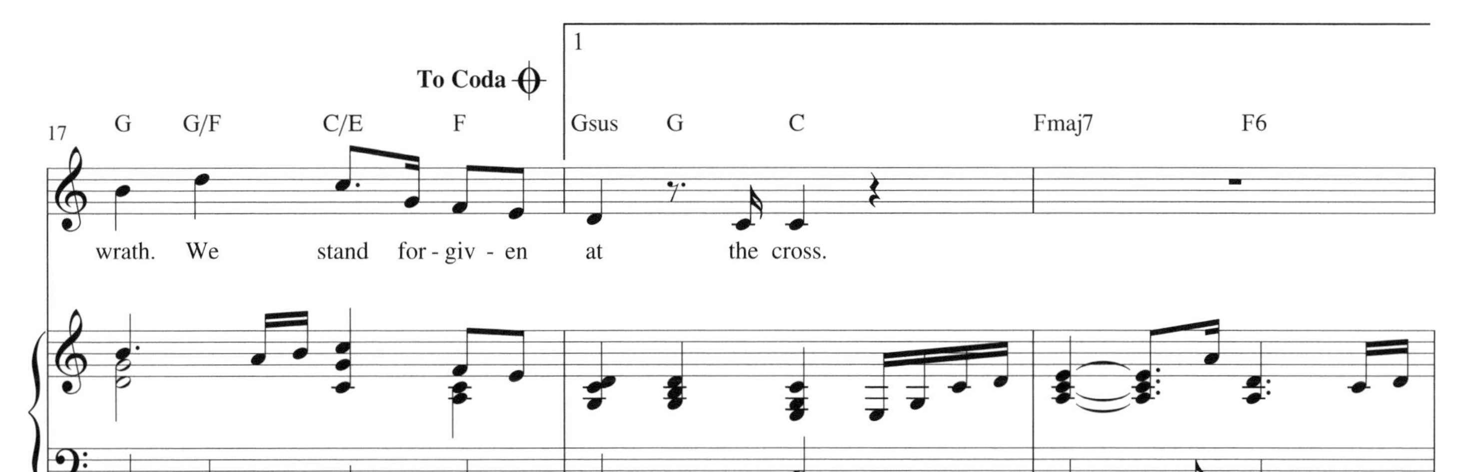
To Coda
1
17
G G/F C/E F Gsus G C Fmaj7 F6
wrath. We stand for-giv-en at the cross.

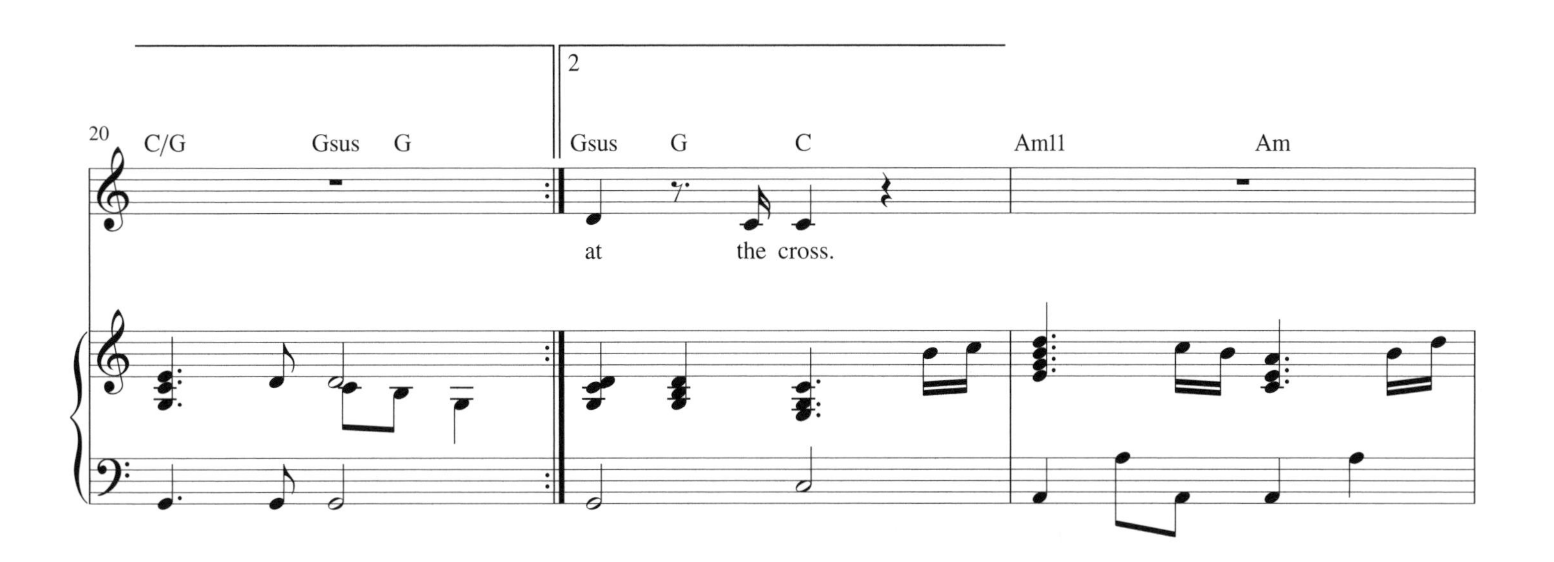
2
20
C/G Gsus G Gsus G C Am11 Am
at the cross.

D.S. al Coda
23
Fmaj7
G
Gsus
G
F/A
G/B

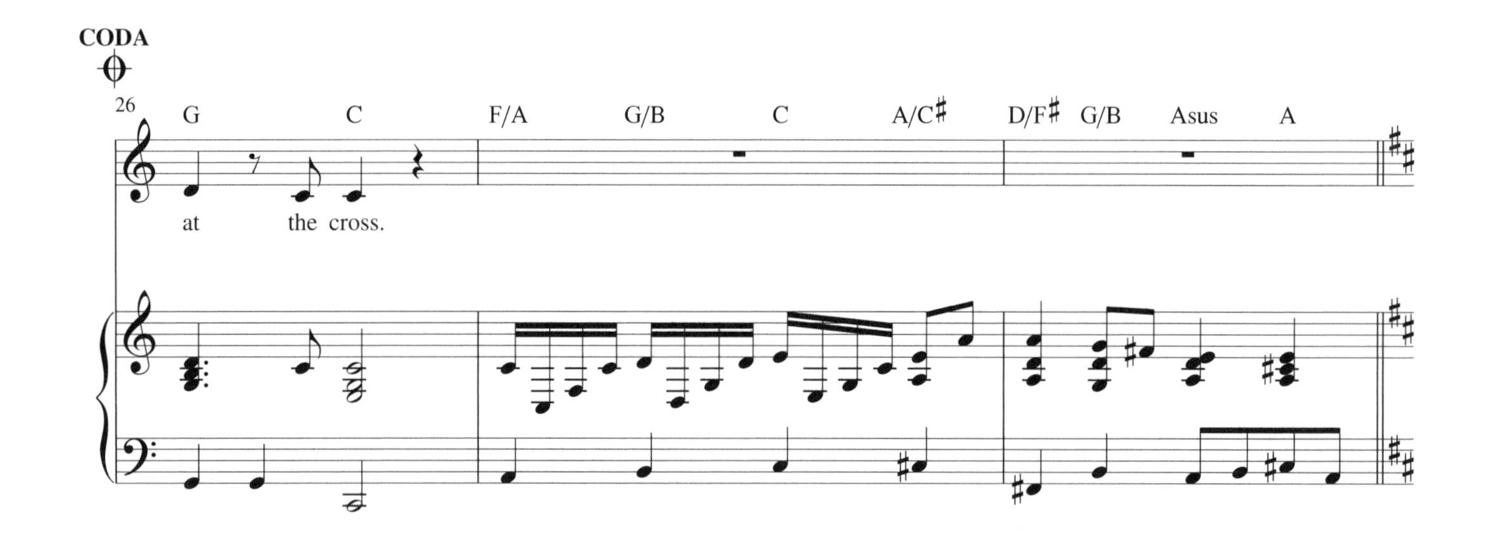
CODA
26
G
C
F/A
G/B
C
A/C♯
D/F♯
G/B
Asus
A
at the cross.

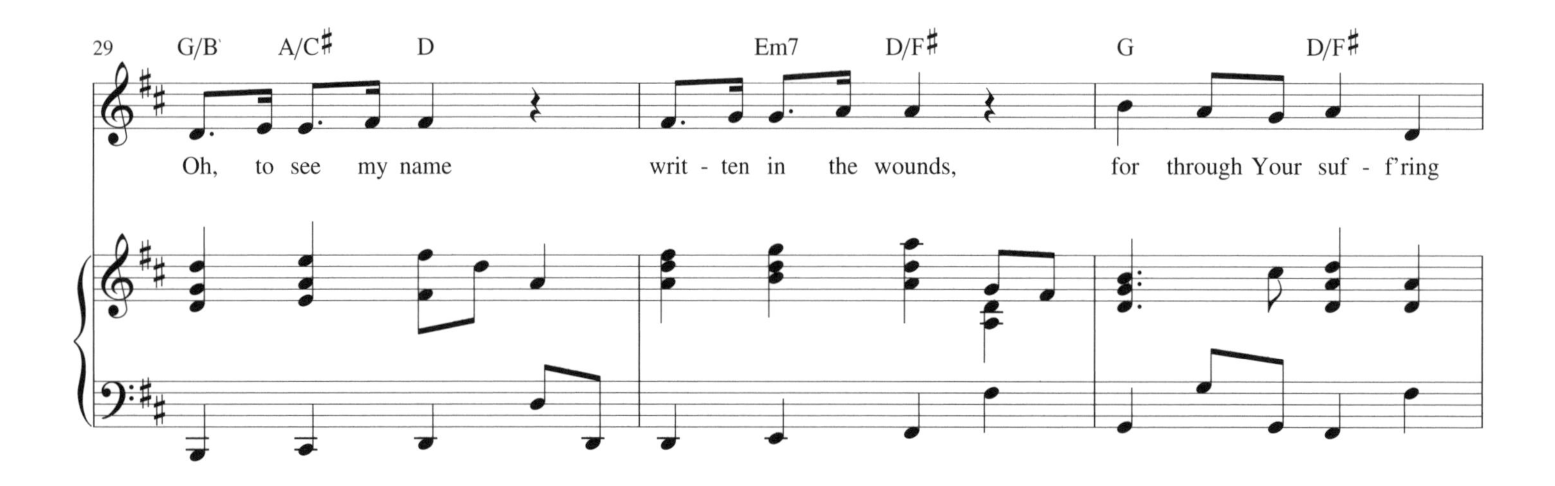
29
G/B
A/C♯
D
Em7
D/F♯
G
D/F♯
Oh, to see my name writ - ten in the wounds, for through Your suf - f'ring

32
Em7
D/G
Asus
A
G/B
A/C♯
D
Em7
D/F♯
I am free. Death is crushed to death, life is mine to live,

35
G D/F♯ Asus A D/F♯ G A/C♯
won through Your self - less love. This, the pow'r of the

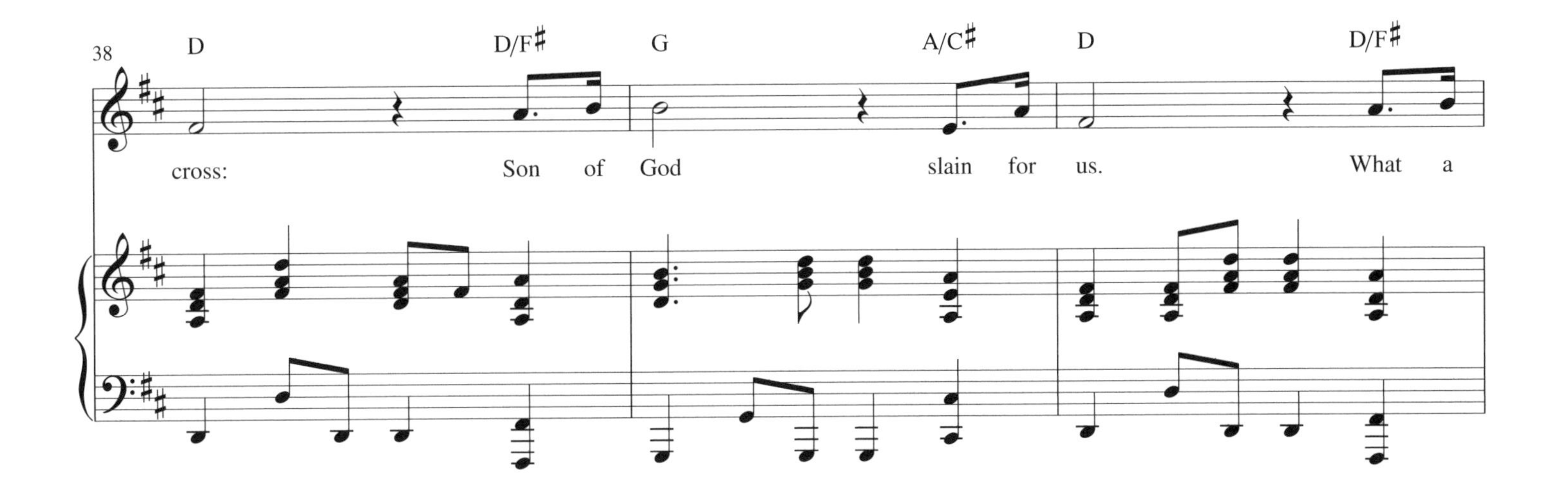
38
D D/F♯ G A/C♯ D D/F♯
cross: Son of God slain for us. What a

41
G E/G♯ A A/G D/F♯ G Asus A
love, what a cost. We stand for-giv - en at the

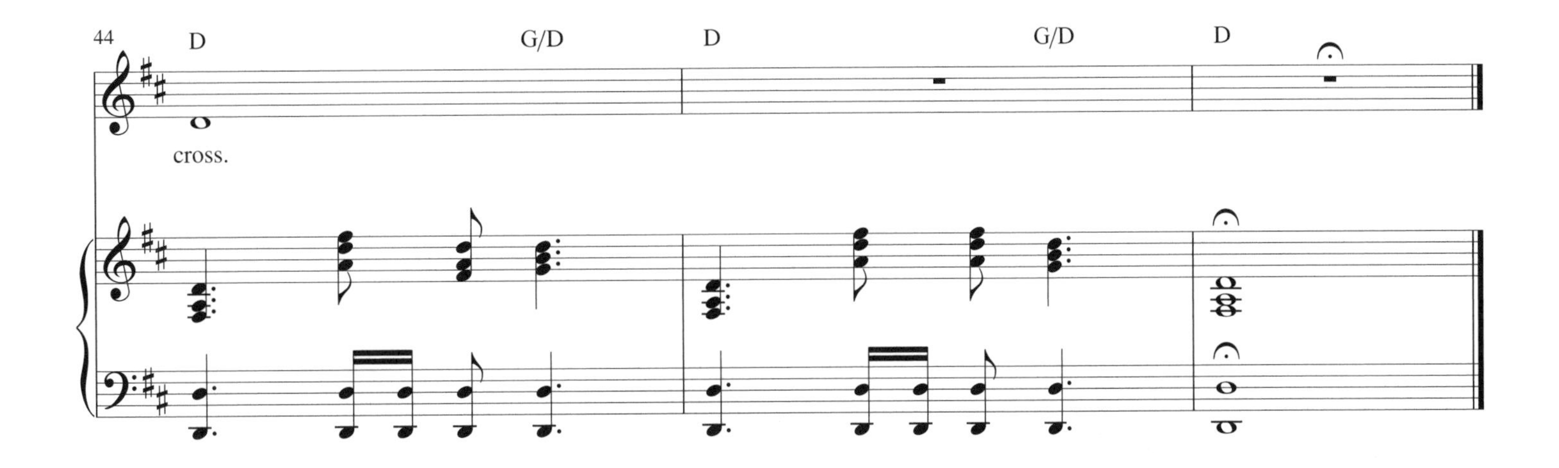
44
D G/D D G/D D
cross.

Revelation Song

Words and Music by
JENNIE LEE RIDDLE

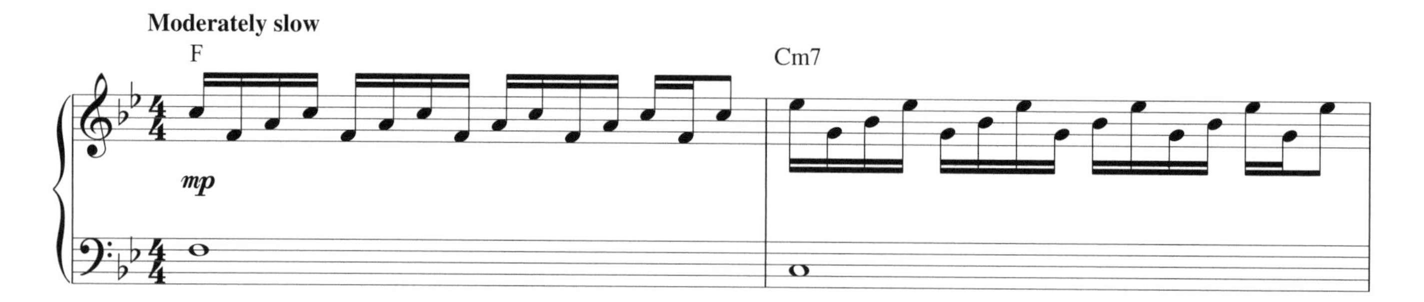

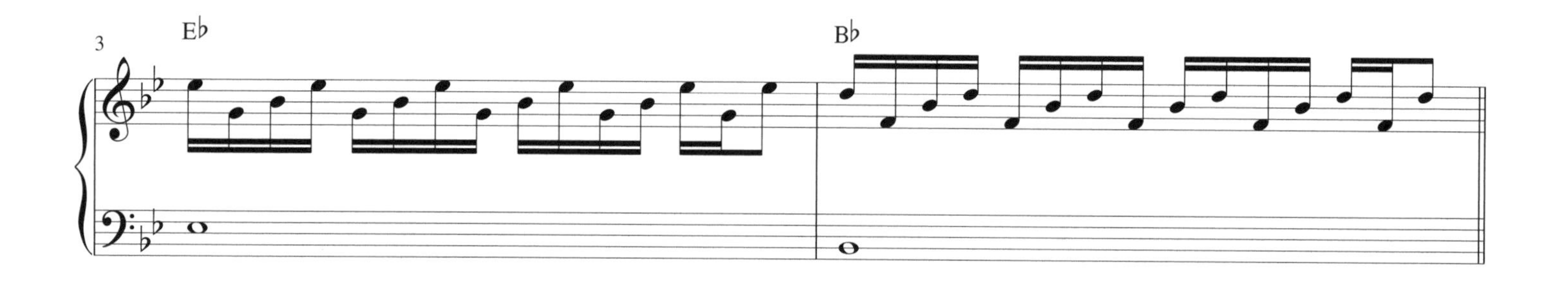

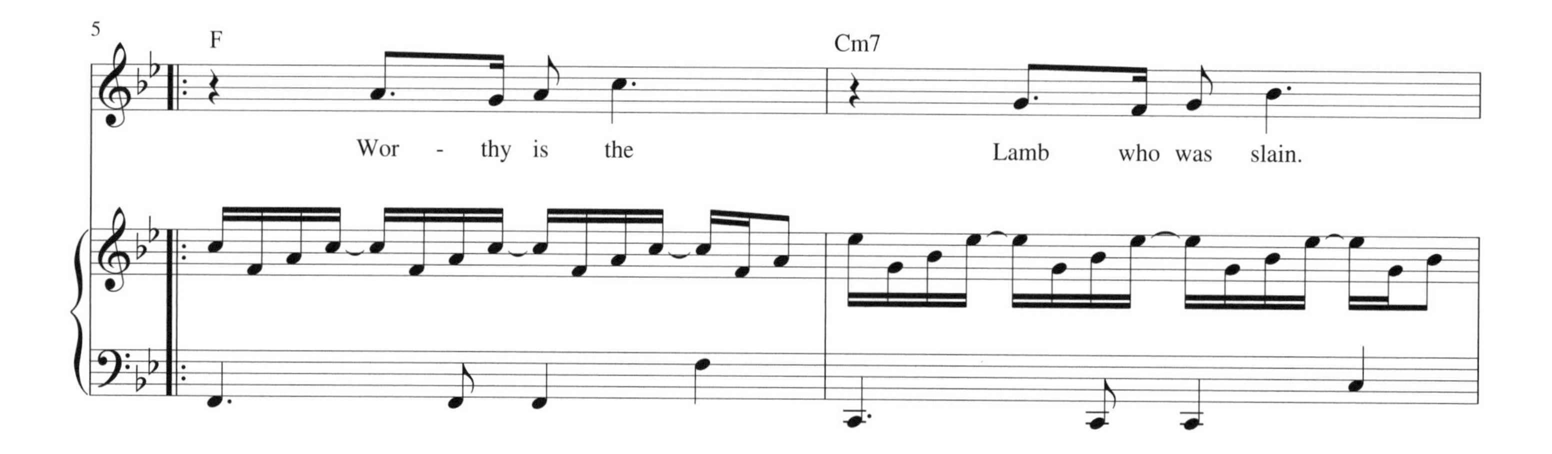

9
F
Cm7
Sing a new song
to Him who sits on

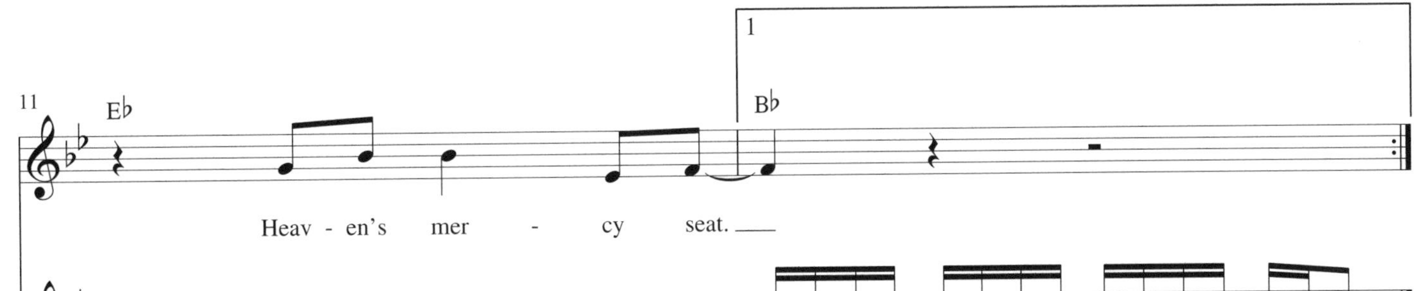
11
E♭
1
B♭
Heav - en's mer - cy seat.

2
13
B♭
F
Ho - ly, ho - ly, ho - ly
mf

15
Cm7
E♭
B♭
is the Lord God Al-might - y,
who was and is and is to come.

18
F
Cm7
E♭
To Coda
With all cre-a-tion, I sing praise to the King of kings. You are my ev-'ry-thing, and

21
B♭
F
Cm7
I will a-dore You. Yeah, I will a-

24
E♭
B♭
F
dore You. Clothed in rain-bows

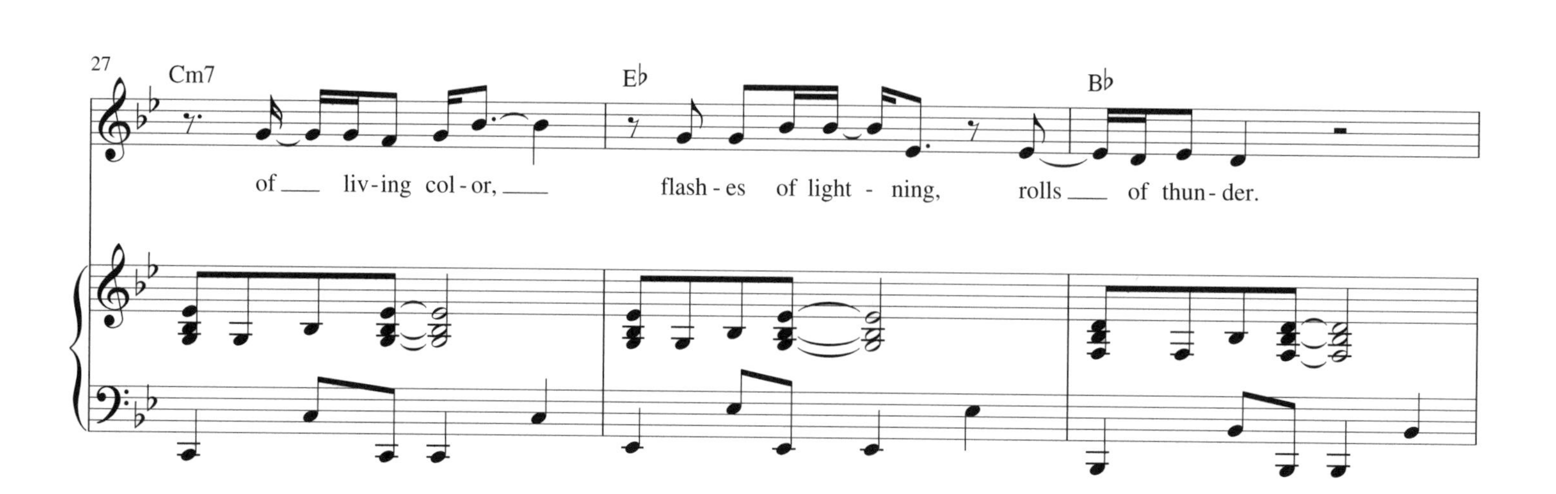
27
Cm7
E♭
B♭
of liv-ing col-or, flash-es of light-ning, rolls of thun-der.

30
F
Cm7
Eb
Bless-ing and hon - or, strength and glo-ry and pow-er be to You, the on - ly wise

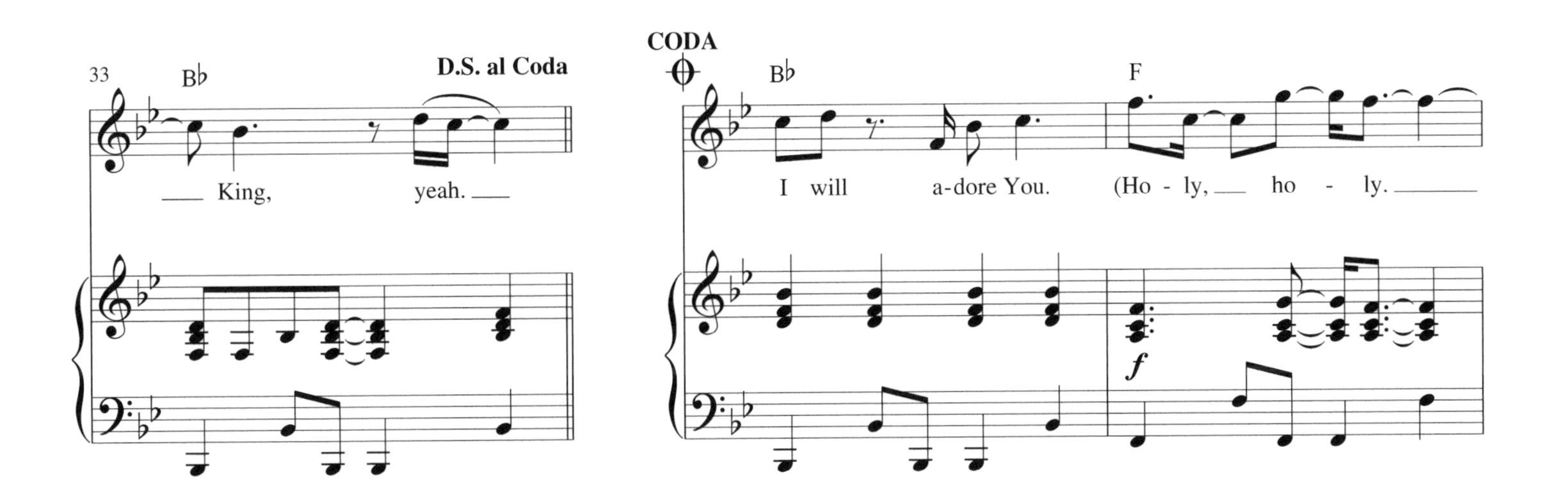
33
Bb
D.S. al Coda
CODA
Bb
F
King, yeah.
I will a-dore You. (Ho - ly, ho - ly.
f

36
Cm7
Eb
Bb
You are ho - ly.)

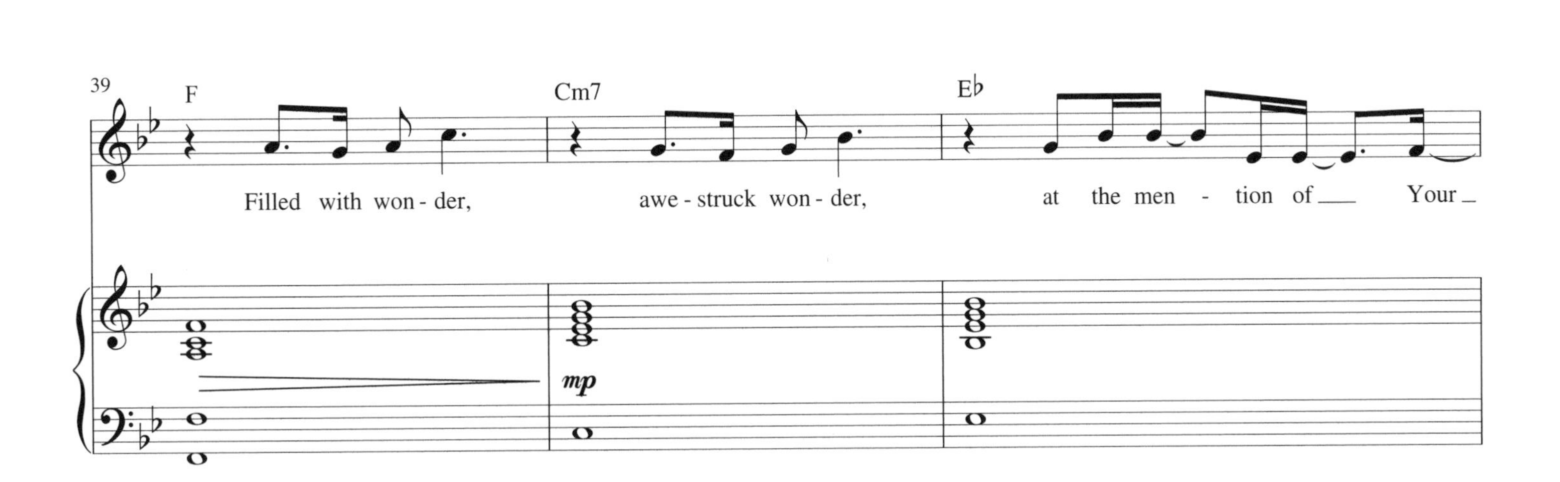
39
F
Cm7
Eb
Filled with won-der, awe-struck won-der, at the men - tion of Your
mp

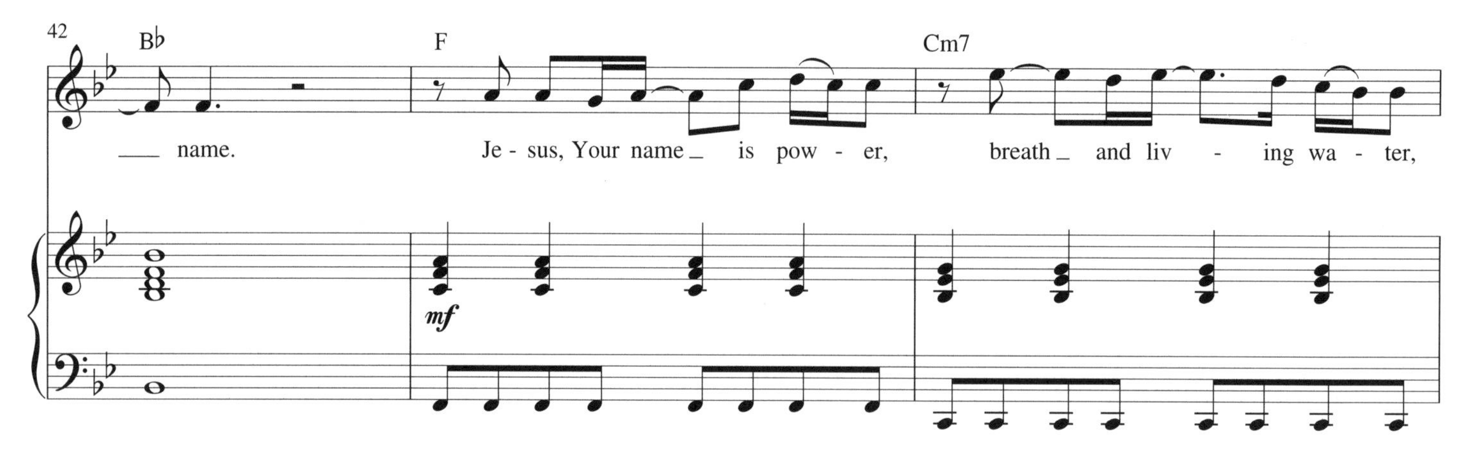
42
B♭
F
Cm7
name.
Je - sus, Your name is pow - er,
breath and liv - ing wa - ter,
mf

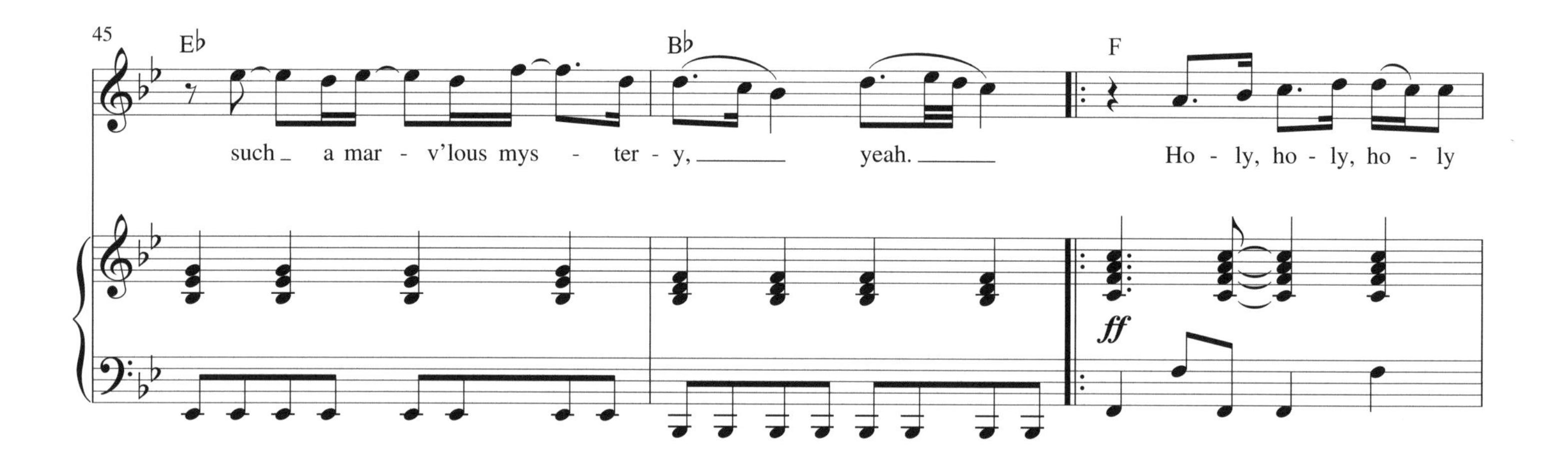
45
E♭
B♭
F
such a mar - v'lous mys - ter - y,
yeah.
Ho - ly, ho - ly, ho - ly
ff

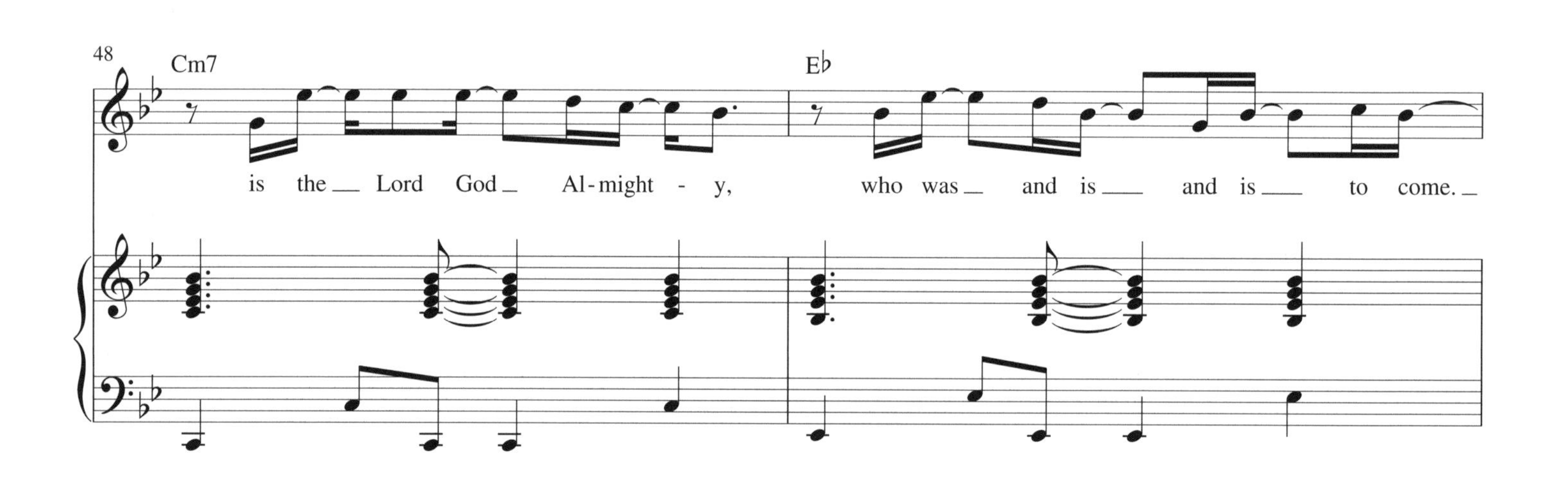
48
Cm7
E♭
is the Lord God Al - might - y,
who was and is and is to come.

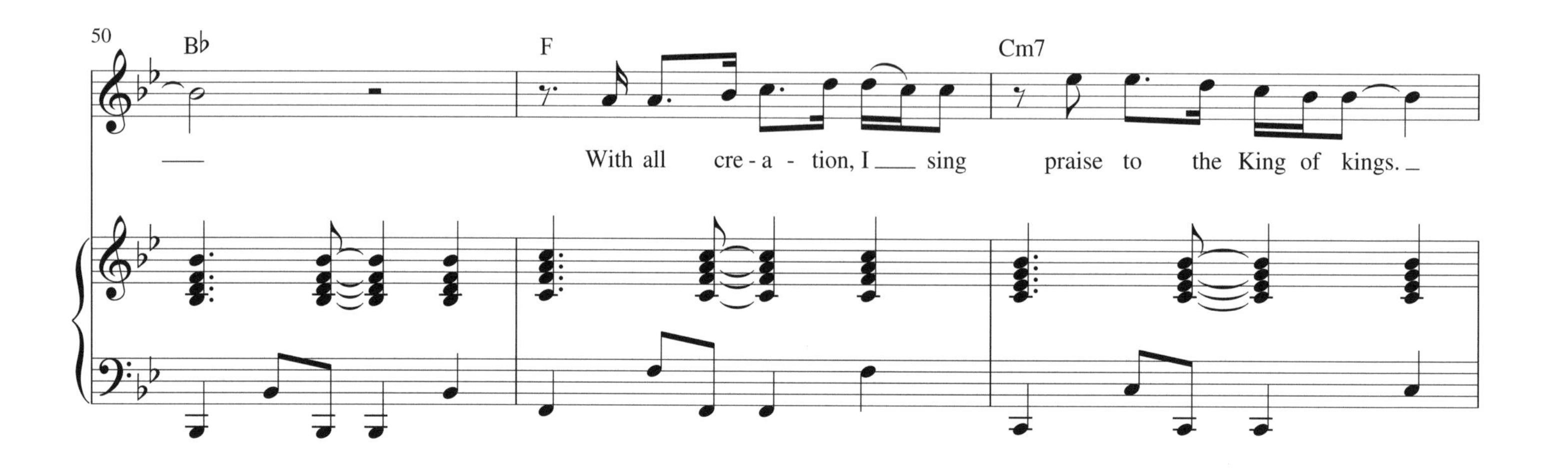
50
B♭
F
Cm7
With all cre - a - tion, I sing
praise to the King of kings.

53
E♭
B♭
B♭
1
2
You are my ev-'ry-thing, and I will a-dore You. I will a-dore You,

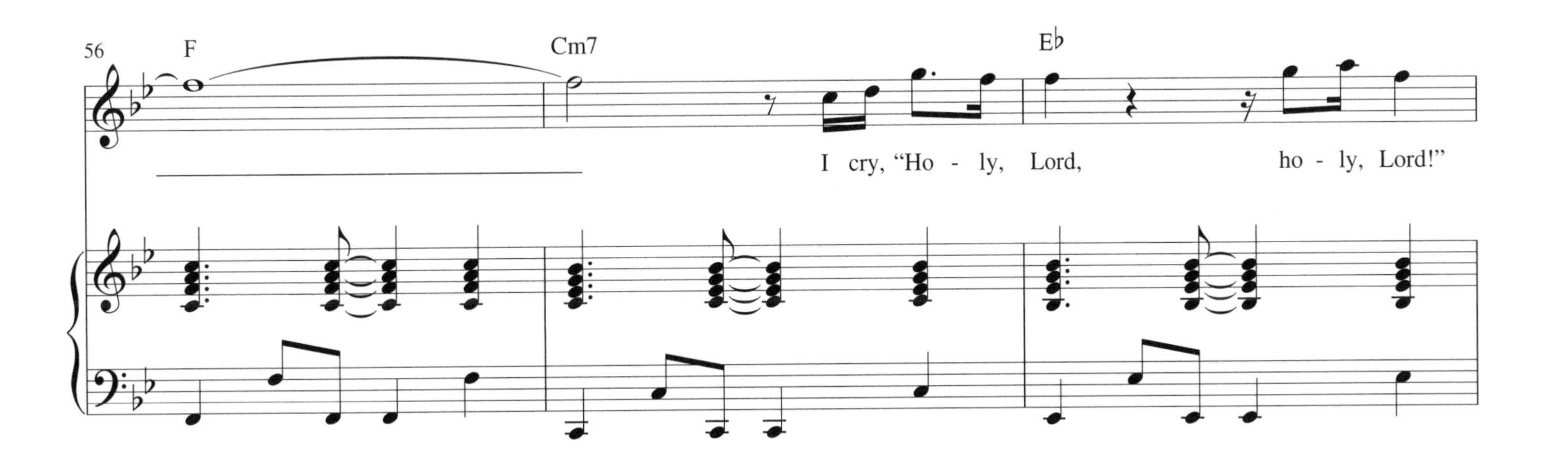
56
F
Cm7
E♭
I cry, "Ho-ly, Lord, ho-ly, Lord!"

59
B♭
F
Cm7
All cre-a-tion sings, "Ho-ly!" (Ho-ly, ho-ly.) Lord, You are ho-ly.

62
E♭
B♭
F
(You are ho-ly.)

Thy Word

Words and Music by MICHAEL W. SMITH
and AMY GRANT

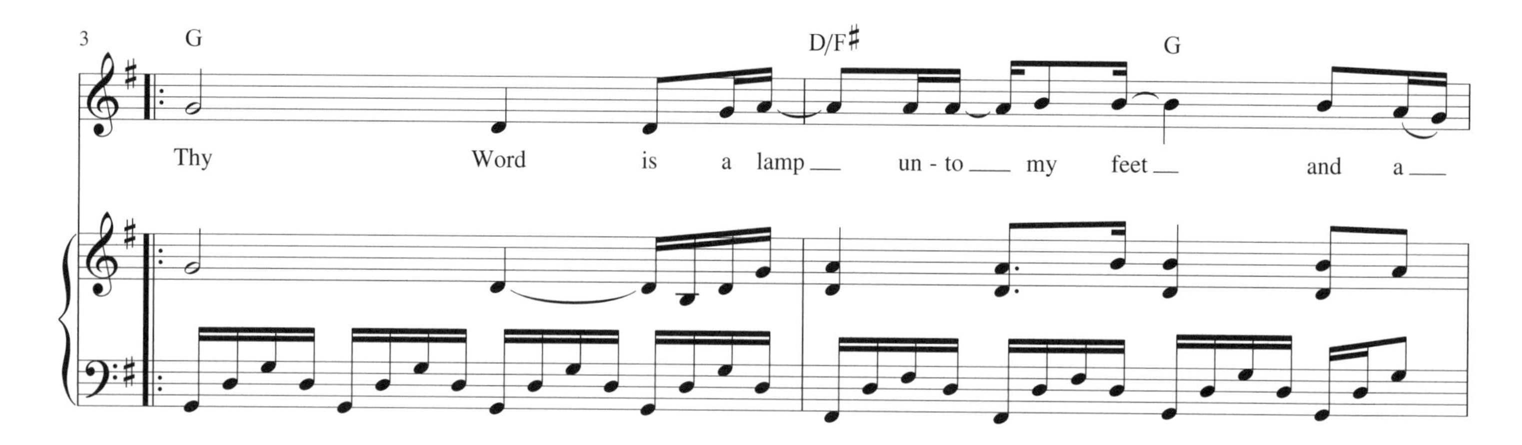

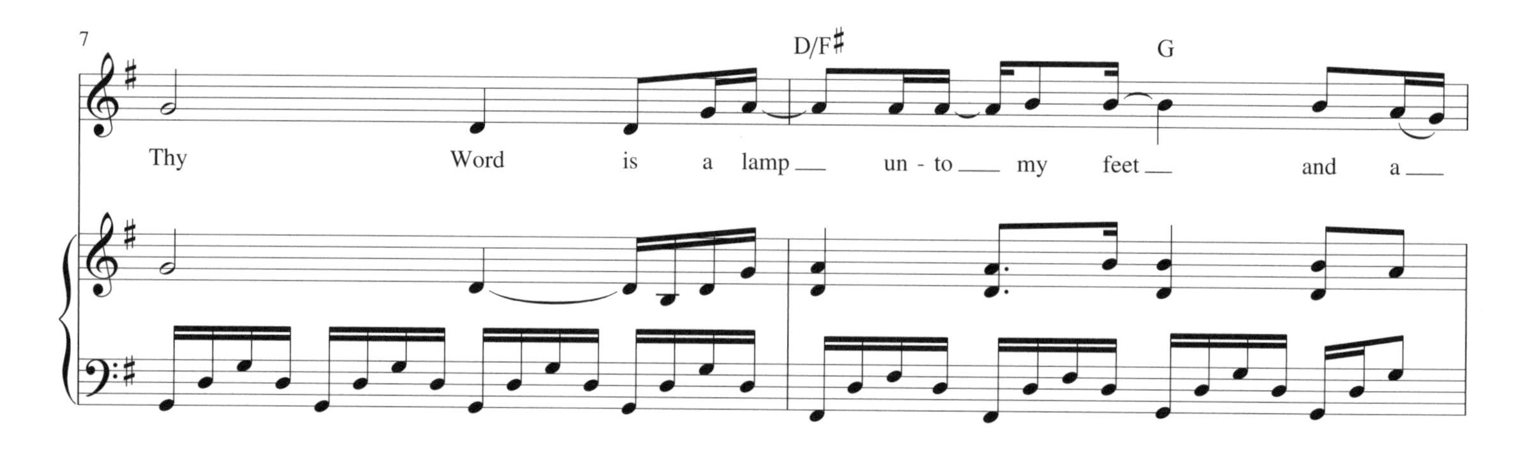

9
C/E
D/F♯
G
light unto my path.
Now

11
D/F♯
Am
Em
Bm
When I feel afraid, think I've lost my way,
I will not forget Your love for me and yet my

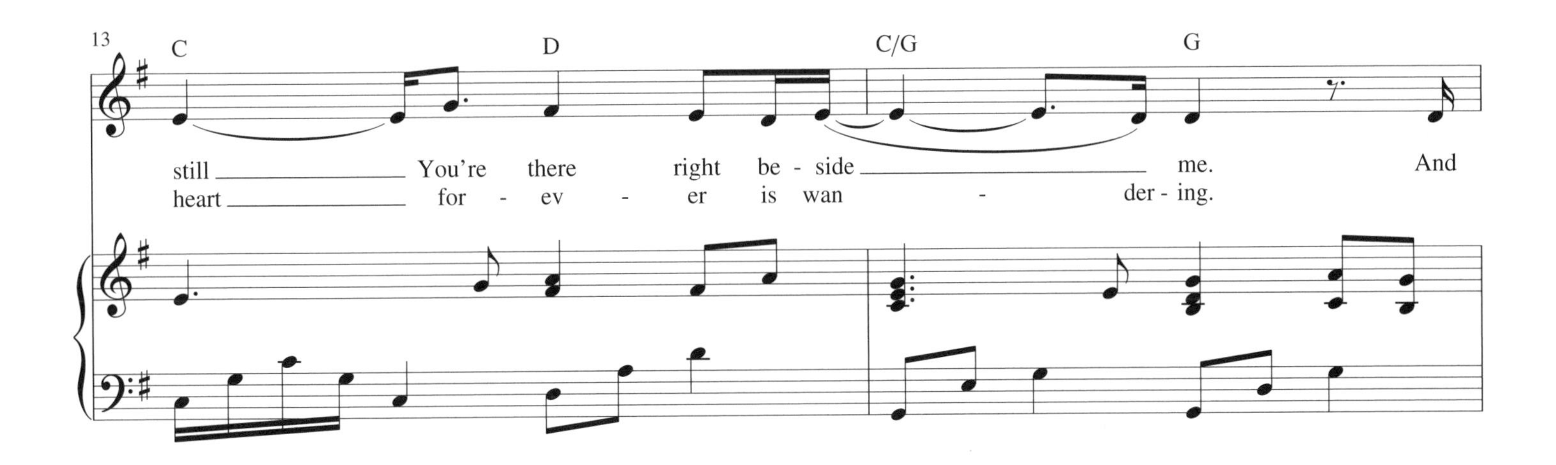
13
C
D
C/G
G
still You're there right beside me. And
heart forever is wandering.

15
D/F♯
Am
Em
Bm
nothing will I fear as long as You are near.
Jesus, be my guide and hold me to Your side, and

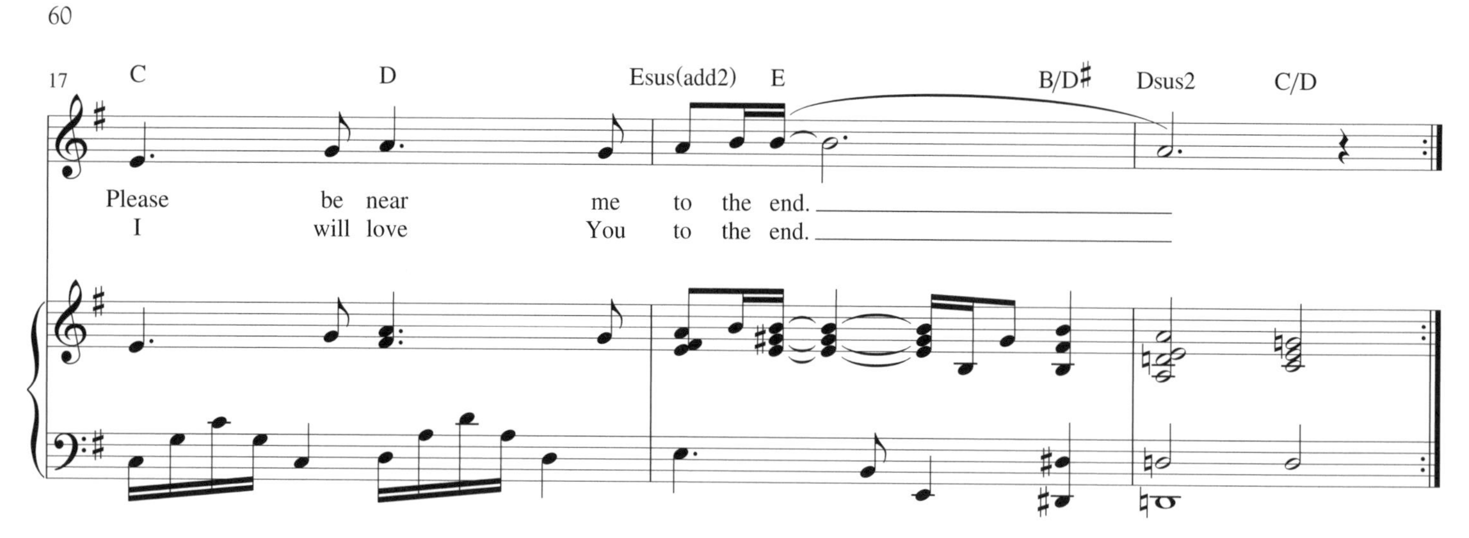
17
C
D
Esus(add2)
E
B/D♯
Dsus2
C/D
Please be near me to the end.
I will love You to the end.

20
G
D/F♯
G

22
C/E
D/F♯
G

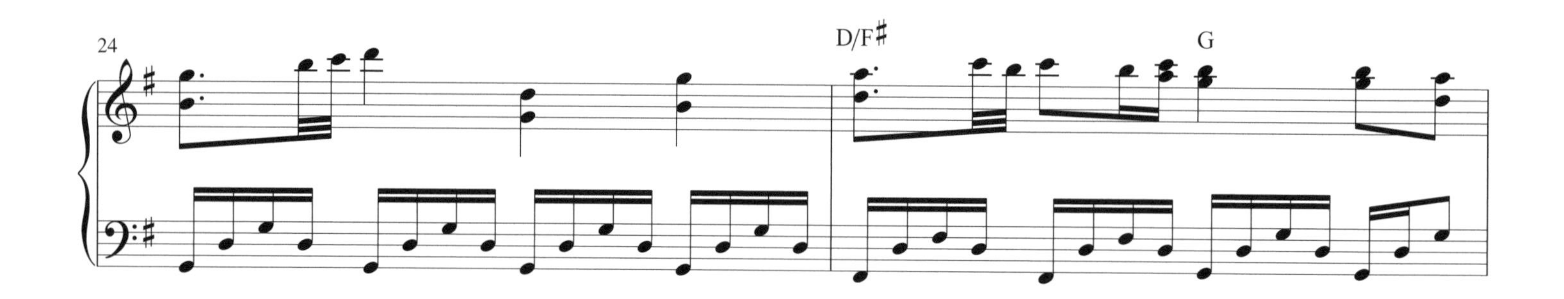
24
D/F♯
G

26
C/E
D/F♯
G

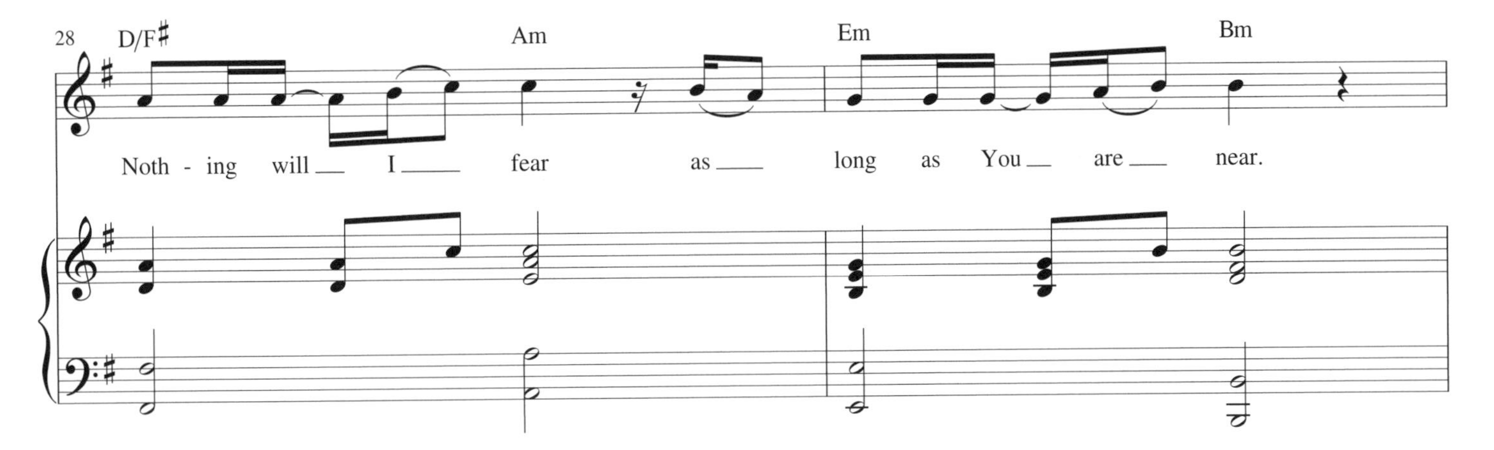
28
D/F♯
Am
Em
Bm
Noth - ing will I fear as long as You are near.

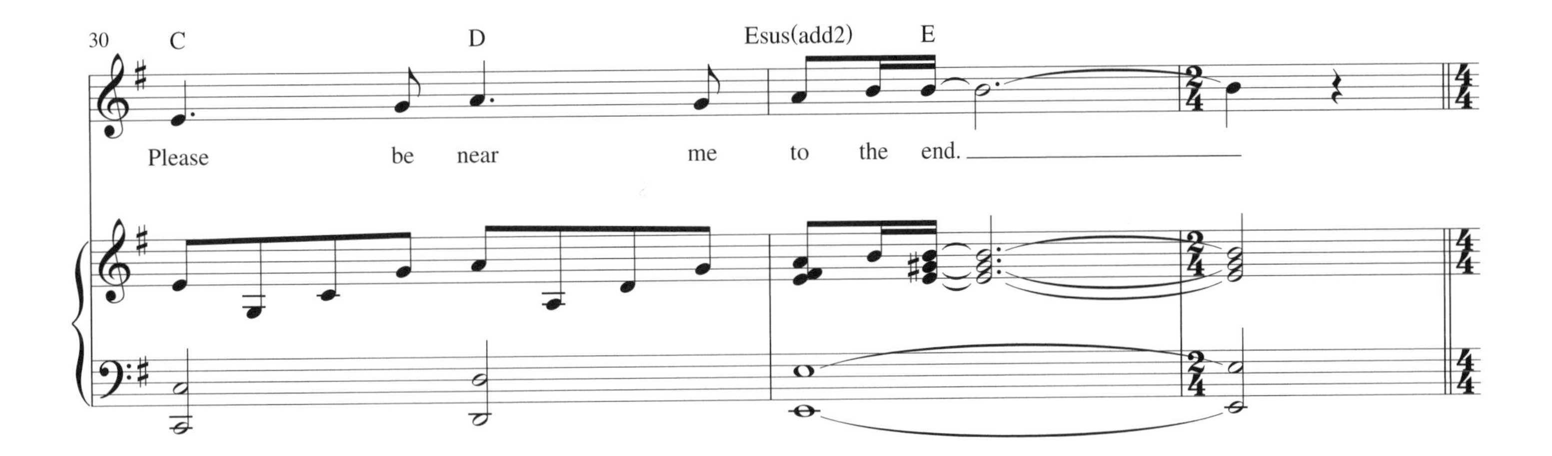
30
C
D
Esus(add2)
E
Please be near me to the end.

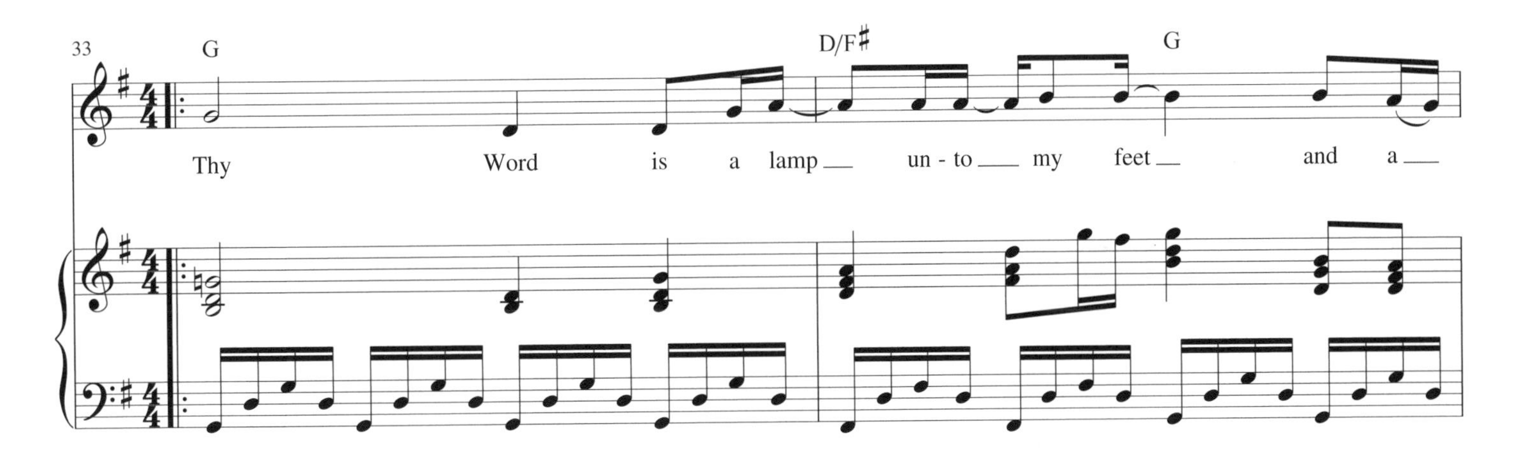
33
G
D/F♯
G
Thy Word is a lamp un - to my feet and a

1
35
C/E
D/F♯
G
light un - to my path.

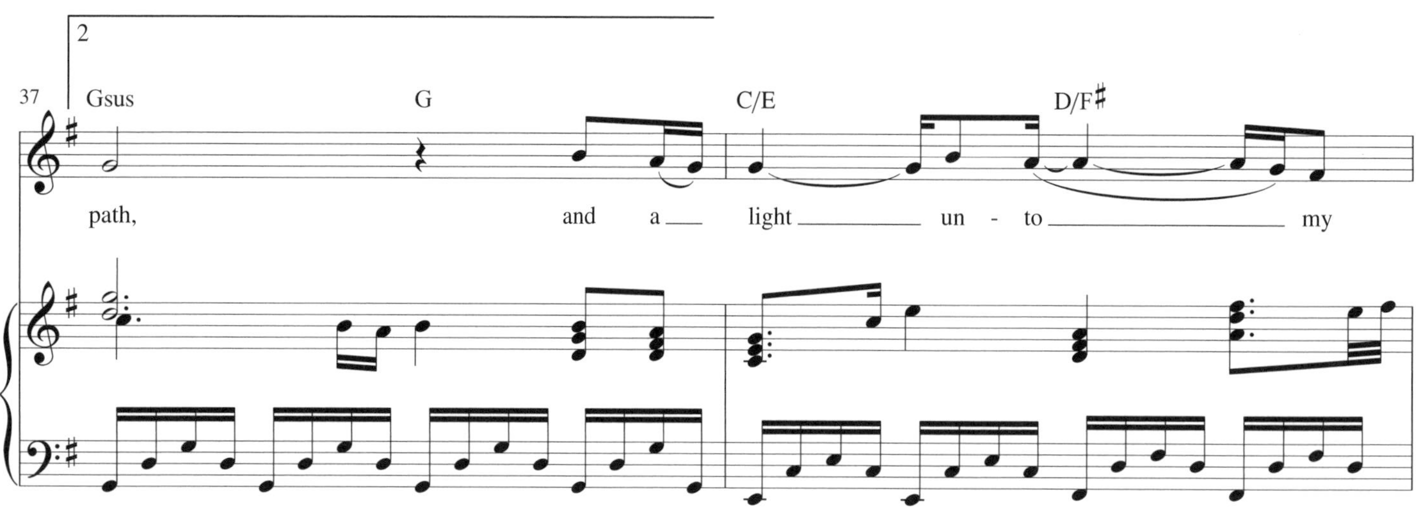
2
37
Gsus
G
C/E
D/F♯
path,
and a
light
un - to
my

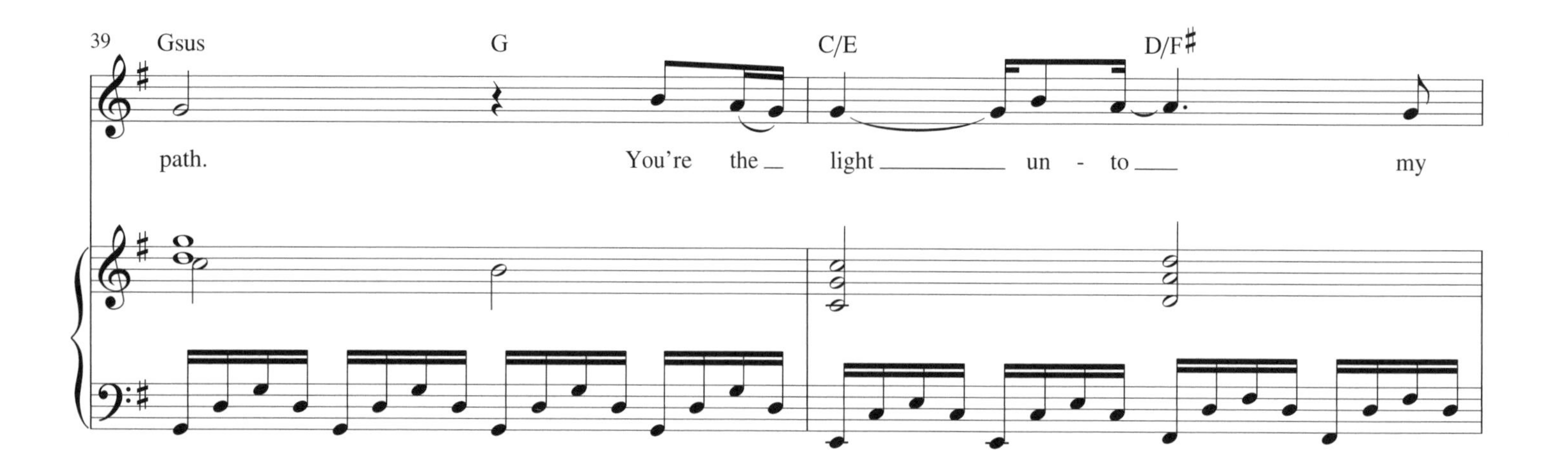
39
Gsus
G
C/E
D/F♯
path.
You're the
light
un - to
my

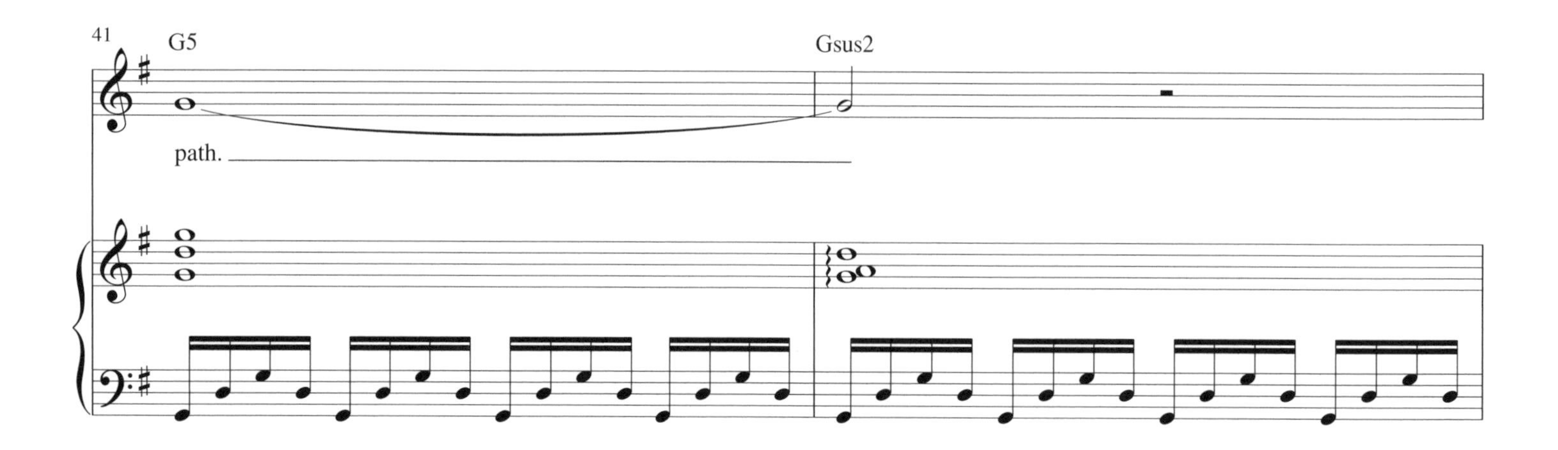
41
G5
Gsus2
path.

43
8va
G(add2)

ABOUT THE ENHANCED CD

In addition to piano accompaniments playable on both your CD player and computer, this enhanced CD also includes tempo adjustment and transposition software for computer use only. This software, known as Amazing Slow Downer, was originally created for use in pop music to allow singers and players the freedom to independently adjust both tempo and pitch elements. Because we believe there may be valuable educational use for these features in classical and theatre music, we have included this software as a tool for both the teacher and student. For quick and easy installation instructions of this software, please see below.

In recording a piano accompaniment we necessarily must choose one tempo. Our choice of tempo, phrasing, ritardandos, and dynamics is carefully considered. But by the nature of recording, it is only one option.

However, we encourage you to explore your own interpretive ideas, which may differ from our recordings. This new software feature allows you to adjust the tempo up and down without affecting the pitch. Likewise, Amazing Slow Downer allows you to shift pitch up and down without affecting the tempo. We recommend that these new tempo and pitch adjustment features be used with care and insight. Ideally, you will be using these recorded accompaniments and Amazing Slow Downer for practice only.

The audio quality may be somewhat compromised when played through the Amazing Slow Downer. This compromise in quality will not be a factor in playing the CD audio track on a normal CD player or through another audio computer program.

INSTALLATION INSTRUCTIONS:

For Macintosh OS 8, 9 and X:

- Load the CD-ROM into your CD-ROM Drive on your computer.
- Each computer is set up a little differently. Your computer may automatically open the audio CD portion of this enhanced CD and begin to play it.
- To access the CD-ROM features, double-click on the data portion of the CD-ROM (which will have the Hal Leonard icon in red and be named as the book).
- Double-click on the "Amazing OS 8 (9 or X)" folder.
- Double-click "Amazing Slow Downer"/"Amazing X PA" to run the software from the CD-ROM, or copy this file to your hard disk and run it from there.
- Follow the instructions on-screen to get started. The Amazing Slow Downer should display tempo, pitch and mix bars. Click to select your track and adjust pitch or tempo by sliding the appropriate bar to the left or to the right.

For Windows:

- Load the CD-ROM into your CD-ROM Drive on your computer.
- Each computer is set up a little differently. Your computer may automatically open the audio CD portion of this enhanced CD and begin to play it.
- To access the CD-ROM features, click on My Computer then right click on the Drive that you placed the CD in. Click Open. You should then see a folder named "Amazing Slow Downer". Click to open the "Amazing Slow Downer" folder.
- Double-click "setup.exe" to install the software from the CD-ROM to your hard disk. Follow the on-screen instructions to complete installation.
- Go to "Start," "Programs" and find the "Amazing Slow Downer" folder. Go to that folder and select the "Amazing Slow Downer" software.
- Follow the instructions on-screen to get started. The Amazing Slow Downer should display tempo, pitch and mix bars. Click to select your track and adjust pitch or tempo by sliding the appropriate bar to the left or to the right.
- Note: On Windows NT, 2000, XP, Vista, and 7, the user should be logged in as the "Administrator" to guarantee access to the CD-ROM drive. Please see the help file for further information.

MINIMUM SYSTEM REQUIREMENTS:

For Macintosh:
Power Macintosh; Mac OS 8.5 or higher, OSX; 4 MB Application RAM; 8x Multi-Session CD-ROM drive

For Windows:
Pentium, Celeron or equivalent processor; Windows 95, 98, ME, NT, 2000, XP, Vista, 7; 4 MB Application RAM; 8x Multi-Session CD-ROM drive